Unlock the Academic Word List: Sublists 7-10

Sheldon Smith

ISBN 978-1-912579-70-9
First Edition

This book is published by Evident Press in conjunction with EAPFoundation.com and EAPCourses.com websites. For more information on titles by Evident Press, visit www.evidentpress.com.

Acknowledgements
Academic collocations are derived from the Academic Collocation List (ACL), developed by Kirsten Ackermann and Yu-Hua Chen using the Pearson International Corpus of Academic English (PICAE). The lists were generated using the online ACL highlighter of EAPFoundation.com. See: http://www.eapfoundation.com/vocab/academic/acl/highlighter/.

The texts used in the Exercises section are taken from the OpenStax resources provided by Rice University. Acknowledgements are given where those texts occur.

Pronunciation of words is adapted from *The Carnegie Mellon University Pronouncing Dictionary*.

Contents

Introduction 5
About the Academic Word List 5
About this book 5
Guidance for study 6
Academic Word List: Sublist 7 7
Exercises (Sublist 7) 42
Task 1: Focus on Meaning #1 42
Task 2: Focus on Meaning #2 44
Task 3: Focus on Meaning #3 45
Task 4: Collocations #1 46
Task 5: Collocations #2 46
Task 6: Word form #1 47
Task 7: Word form #2 48
Academic Word List: Sublist 8 49
Exercises (Sublist 8) 80
Task 1: Focus on Meaning #1 80
Task 2: Focus on Meaning #2 81
Task 3: Focus on Meaning #3 83
Task 4: Collocations #1 84
Task 5: Collocations #2 84
Task 6: Word form #1 85
Task 7: Word form #2 86
Academic Word List: Sublist 9 87
Exercises (Sublist 9) 118
Task 1: Focus on Meaning #1 118
Task 2: Focus on Meaning #2 120
Task 3: Focus on Meaning #3 122
Task 4: Collocations #1 123
Task 5: Collocations #2 123
Task 6: Word form #1 124
Task 7: Word form #2 125
Academic Word List: Sublist 10 127
Exercises (Sublist 10) 143
Task 1: Focus on Meaning #1 143
Task 2: Focus on Meaning #2 145
Task 3: Collocations 146

Task 4: Word form 146
Answers to exercises 147
Sublist 7....................147
Sublist 8....................153
Sublist 9....................158
Sublist 10....................165
Index of words 168
About the author 174
Accessing Online Resources 175

Introduction

About the Academic Word List

The Academic Word List (AWL) was developed by Averil Coxhead at Victoria University of Wellington, New Zealand. The list contains 570 word families which frequently appear in academic texts, but which are not contained in the General Service List (GSL). The 570 word families of the AWL are divided into 10 lists (called sublists) according to how frequent they are. Sublist 1 has the most frequent word families, sublist 2 the next most frequent word families, up to sublist 10, which has the least frequent. Each sublist contains 60 word families, except for sublist 10, which only has 30.

About this book

The book has the following features.

1) All words in each AWL sublist are given.
2) Pronunciation of each headword is shown.
3) Definitions are given for each headword. These are the most common definitions of these words, rather than all possible meanings (many meanings of the words do not relate to how they are used in academic contexts).
4) The word family of each word is also given (adj, noun, verb, etc.). These are categorised by type, so you can easily tell which word has which word form.
5) Common academic collocations using each AWL word are also given. These are taken from the ACL (Academic Collocations List) developed by Pearson Education.
6) There are exercises at the end of each sublist to help you practise each of the words. The exercises cover **all 60 words in each sublist** (all 30 for sublist 10), often multiple times. More exercises can be found by accessing the online resources. See the end of the book for access details.
7) There is a study guide (below) to help you understand how to use the AWL, and this book, to improve your academic vocabulary.
8) For the sake of clarity, each word is shown either on a single page, or with two words occupying one page.

Guidance for study

When studying vocabulary, the first step is to understand the *meaning*. Looking up words in a dictionary to find the meaning can be difficult, and so to help you with this, all headwords in the book have definitions, which are limited to how the words are used in academic contexts.

Many students simply never get past the first step, which means they may be able to understand the word when reading, but will not be able to use it *productively* in writing or speaking. A second step is to understand different word forms of the word, i.e. the word family. This will enable you to use the word more flexibly in your speaking or writing, and is an especially useful skill if you want to paraphrase material. For example, the word *contrast*, in AWL sublist 4, can be a *verb* or *noun*. The *adjective* form is *contrasting* or *contrastive*.

A third step is to focus on usage. Here you would need a good dictionary to help, or you can study the word in context. This book helps by giving example sentences, though these are only of the headword, and further study may be needed. Examples of usage for the word *convert* are shown below.

convert (v) from [A] to [B]	*It was converted from traditional to modern style.*
[A] convert (v) into [B]	*Many public schools are converting into private ones.*
convert (n) to [sth]	*He became a convert to the new theory.*

Also related to usage are collocations, or common word combinations. This book includes all collocations from the ACL (Academic Collocations List) which use these words.

A fourth step is to focus on pronunciation. Understanding the pronunciation of a word is important if you want to use the word correctly in your speaking, or understand it in a lecture. Pay particular attention to shifting stress as the word form changes. For example, the noun form CONvert has the stress on the first syllable, while the verb form conVERT has the stress on the second syllable. Note that only pronunciation of headword is given in this book, so for this extended pronunciation work you would need to use a dictionary.

Academic Word List:

Sublist 7

adapt

[ədæpt]

verb

1. adapt or conform oneself to new or different conditions. [Syn: *adjust*, *conform*]

n (thing)	verb	adj	opposite
adaptability adaptation	adapt	adaptable adapted adaptive	x
n (person)	**verb forms**	**adv**	**other**
x	adapted adapting adapts	x	x

---

adult

[ədʌlt]

adj

1. (of animals) fully developed. E.g.: **an adult animal** [Syn: *big*, *full-grown*, *fully grown*, *grown*, *grownup*]

noun

1. a fully developed person from maturity onward. [Syn: *grownup*]
2. any mature animal.

n (thing)	verb	adj	opposite
adult adulthood	x	adult	x
n (person)	**verb forms**	**adv**	**other**
x	x	x	x

advocate

[ædvəkət]

verb

1. speak, plead, or argue in favour of. E.g.: **The doctor advocated a smoking ban in the entire house** [Syn: *preach*]

noun

1. a person who pleads for a cause or propounds an idea. [Syn: *advocator*, *proponent*, *exponent*]

n (thing)	**verb**	**adj**	**opposite**
advocacy	advocate	x	x
n (person)	**verb forms**	**adv**	**other**
advocate	advocated advocates advocating	x	x

---

aid

[eɪd]

verb

1. give help or assistance; be of service. [Syn: *help*, *assist*]

noun

1. a gift of money to support a worthy person or cause. [Syn: *economic aid*]
2. a resource. E.g.: **visual aids in teaching** [Syn: *assistance*, *help*]
3. the work of caring for or attending to someone or something. [Syn: *care*, *attention*, *tending*]

n (thing)	**verb**	**adj**	**opposite**
aid	aid	x	unaided
n (person)	**verb forms**	**adv**	**other**
x	aided aiding aids	x	x

channel

[tʃænəl]

verb

1. transmit or serve as the medium for transmission. [Syn: *conduct*, *transmit*, *convey*, *carry*]
2. direct the flow of. E.g.: **channel information towards a broad audience** [Syn: *canalize*, *canalise*]

noun

1. a long narrow furrow cut either by a natural process (such as erosion) or by a tool (as e.g. a groove in a phonograph record). [Syn: *groove*]
2. a deep and relatively narrow body of water (as in a river or a harbor or a strait linking two larger bodies) that allows the best passage for vessels. E.g.: **the ship went aground in the channel**
3. a passage for water (or other fluids) to flow through. E.g.: **the fields were crossed with irrigation channels, gutters carried off the rainwater into a series of channels under the street**
4. a television station and its programs. E.g.: **a satellite TV channel, surfing through the channels, they offer more than one hundred channels** [Syn: *television channel*, *TV channel*]
5. a way of selling a company's product either directly or via distributors. E.g.: **possible distribution channels are wholesalers or small retailers or retail chains or direct mailers or your own stores** [Syn: *distribution channel*]

n (thing)	**verb**	**adj**	**opposite**
channel	channel	x	x
n (person)	**verb forms**	**adv**	**other**
x	channelled channelling channels	x	x

chemical

[kemɪkəl]

adj

1. relating to or used in chemistry. E.g.: **chemical engineer**, **chemical balance** [Syn: *chemic*]
2. of or made from or using substances produced by or used in reactions involving atomic or molecular changes. E.g.: **chemical fertilizer**

noun

1. produced by or used in a reaction involving changes in atoms or molecules.

n (thing)	**verb**	**adj**	**opposite**
chemical	x	chemical	x
n (person)	**verb forms**	**adv**	**other**
x	x	chemically	x

---

classic

[klæsɪk]

adj

1. adhering to established standards and principles. E.g.: **a classic proof**
2. characteristic of the classical artistic and literary traditions.

noun

1. a creation of the highest excellence.

n (thing)	**verb**	**adj**	**opposite**
classic classics	x	classic classical	x
n (person)	**verb forms**	**adv**	**other**
x	x	x	x

Collocations from the ACL

adj+n: classic example, classic study, classic text, classic work, classical theory.

comprehensive

[kɑmprihensɪv]

adj

1. broad in scope. E.g.: **a comprehensive survey of world affairs**
2. including all or everything. E.g.: **comprehensive coverage, a comprehensive history of the revolution, a comprehensive survey, a comprehensive education**

n (thing)	verb	adj	opposite
x	x	comprehensive	x
n (person)	**verb forms**	**adv**	**other**
x	x	comprehensively	x

Collocations from the ACL

adj+n: comprehensive account, comprehensive approach, comprehensive overview, comprehensive review, comprehensive system.

----

comprise

[kəmpraɪz]

verb

1. be composed of. E.g.: **The land he conquered comprised several provinces** [Syn: *consist*]

n (thing)	verb	adj	opposite
x	comprise	x	x
n (person)	**verb forms**	**adv**	**other**
x	comprised comprises comprising	x	x

confirm

[kənfɜrm]

verb

1. establish or strengthen as with new evidence or facts. E.g.: **his story confirmed my doubts** [Syn: *corroborate, sustain, substantiate, support, affirm*]

n (thing)	verb	adj	opposite
confirmation	confirm	x	x
n (person)	**verb forms**	**adv**	**other**
x	confirmed confirming confirms	x	x

----

contrary

[kɑntreri]

adj

1. of words or propositions so related that both cannot be true but both may be false. E.g.: **`hot' and `cold' are contrary terms**
2. very opposed in nature or character or purpose. E.g.: **acts contrary to our code of ethics, the facts point to a contrary conclusion**

n (thing)	verb	adj	opposite
x	x	contrary	x
n (person)	**verb forms**	**adv**	**other**
x	x	contrarily	x

convert

[kanv3rt]

verb

1. change from one system to another or to a new plan or policy. E.g.: **We converted from 220 to 110 Volt** [Syn: *change over*]
2. make (someone) agree, understand, or realize the truth or validity of something. [Syn: *win over*, *convince*]
3. change the nature, purpose, or function of something. E.g.: **convert lead into gold, convert hotels into jails, convert slaves to laborers**
4. exchange or replace with another, usually of the same kind or category. E.g.: **Could you convert my dollars into pounds?, convert centimeters into inches, convert holdings into shares** [Syn: *change*, *exchange*, *commute*]

noun

1. a person who has been converted to another religious or political belief.

n (thing)	**verb**	**adj**	**opposite**
conversion	convert	convertible	x
n (person)	**verb forms**	**adv**	**other**
convert	converted converting converts	x	x

couple

[kʌpəl]

verb

1. bring two objects, ideas, or people together. E.g.: **This fact is coupled to the other one** [Syn: *match, mate, pair, twin*]

noun

1. two items of the same kind. [Syn: *pair, twosome, twain, brace, span, yoke, couplet, distich, duo, duet, dyad, duad*]
2. a small indefinite number. E.g.: **he's coming for a couple of days**

n (thing)	**verb**	**adj**	**opposite**
couple	couple	x	x
n (person)	**verb forms**	**adv**	**other**
x	coupled couples coupling	x	x

----

decade

[dekeɪd]

noun

1. a period of 10 years. [Syn: *decennary, decennium*]

n (thing)	**verb**	**adj**	**opposite**
decade	x	x	x
n (person)	**verb forms**	**adv**	**other**
x	x	x	x

Collocations from the ACL

adj+n: next decade, previous decade, early decades, recent decades.

definite

[defənət]

adj

1. precise; explicit and clearly defined. E.g.: **I want a definite answer, a definite statement of the terms of the will, a definite amount, definite restrictions on the sale of alcohol, the wedding date is now definite, a definite drop in attendance**
2. known for certain. E.g.: **it is definite that they have won**

n (thing)	**verb**	**adj**	**opposite**
x	x	definite definitive	indefinite indefinitely
n (person)	**verb forms**	**adv**	**other**
x	x	definitely	x

---

deny

[dɪnaɪ]

verb

1. refuse to let have. [Syn: *refuse*]
2. refuse to accept or believe.
3. refuse to recognize or acknowledge.

n (thing)	**verb**	**adj**	**opposite**
denial	deny	deniable	undeniable
n (person)	**verb forms**	**adv**	**other**
x	denied denies denying	x	x

differentiate

[dɪfɜrenʃieɪt]

verb

1. mark as different. [Syn: *distinguish, separate, secern, secernate, severalize, severalise, tell, tell apart*]
2. become different during development. E.g.: **cells differentiate**

n (thing)	**verb**	**adj**	**opposite**
differentiation	differentiate	differentiated	x
n (person)	**verb forms**	**adv**	**other**
x	differentiated differentiates differentiating	x	x

---

dispose

[dɪspoʊz]

verb

1. throw or cast away. [Syn: *discard, fling, toss, toss out, toss away, chuck out, cast aside, throw out, cast out, throw away, cast away, put away*]
2. give, sell, or transfer to another. E.g.: **She disposed of her parents' possessions**

n (thing)	**verb**	**adj**	**opposite**
disposal	dispose	disposable	x
n (person)	**verb forms**	**adv**	**other**
x	disposed disposes disposing	x	x

dynamic

[daɪnæmɪk]

adj

1. of or relating to dynamics.
2. characterized by action or forcefulness or force of personality. E.g.: **a dynamic market, a dynamic speaker, the dynamic president of the firm** [Syn: *dynamical*]

n (thing)	**verb**	**adj**	**opposite**
dynamics	x	dynamic	x
n (person)	**verb forms**	**adv**	**other**
x	x	dynamically	x

Collocations from the ACL

adj+n: dynamic equilibrium, dynamic nature, dynamic process, dynamic system.

---

eliminate

[ɪlɪməneɪt]

verb

1. do away with. [Syn: *obviate, rid of*]
2. dismiss from consideration. E.g.: **This possibility can be eliminated from our consideration** [Syn: *rule out, reject*]

n (thing)	**verb**	**adj**	**opposite**
elimination	eliminate	x	x
n (person)	**verb forms**	**adv**	**other**
x	eliminated eliminates eliminating	x	x

empirical

[empɪrɪkəl]

adj

1. derived from experiment and observation rather than theory. E.g.: **an empirical basis for an ethical theory, empirical laws, empirical data, an empirical treatment of a disease about which little is known** [Syn: *empiric*]

n (thing)	**verb**	**adj**	**opposite**
empiricism	x	empirical	x
n (person)	**verb forms**	**adv**	**other**
x	x	empirically	x

<u>Collocations from the ACL</u>

adj+n: empirical data, empirical evidence, empirical investigation, empirical research, empirical study, empirical support, empirical work.

----

equip

[ɪkwɪp]

verb

1. provide with (something) usually for a specific purpose. E.g.: **The expedition was equipped with proper clothing, food, and other necessities** [Syn: *fit, fit out, outfit*]

n (thing)	**verb**	**adj**	**opposite**
equipment	equip	equipped	x
n (person)	**verb forms**	**adv**	**other**
x	equipped equipping equips	x	x

extract

[ekstrækt]

verb

1. draw or pull out, usually with some force or effort; also used in an abstract sense. E.g.: **extract a bad tooth, extract information from the telegram** [Syn: *pull out*, *pull*, *pull up*, *take out*, *draw out*]
2. obtain from a substance, as by mechanical action. [Syn: *press out*, *express*]
3. take out of a literary work in order to cite or copy. [Syn: *excerpt*, *take out*]

noun

1. a passage selected from a larger work. [Syn: *excerpt*, *selection*]

n (thing)	**verb**	**adj**	**opposite**
extract extraction	extract	x	x
n (person)	**verb forms**	**adv**	**other**
x	extracted extracting extracts	x	x

<u>Collocations from the ACL</u>

v+n: extract data, extract information.

file

[faɪl]

verb
1. proceed in line. E.g.: **The students filed into the classroom**
2. place in a container for keeping records. [Syn: *file away*]

noun
1. a line of persons or things ranged one behind the other. [Syn: *single file, Indian file*]
2. a set of related records (either written or electronic) kept together. [Syn: *data file*]
3. office furniture consisting of a container for keeping papers in order. [Syn: *file cabinet, filing cabinet*]

n (thing)	**verb**	**adj**	**opposite**
file	file	x	x
n (person)	**verb forms**	**adv**	**other**
x	filed files filing	x	x

----

finite

[faɪnaɪt]

adj
1. bounded or limited in magnitude or spatial or temporal extent.

n (thing)	**verb**	**adj**	**opposite**
x	x	finite	infinite infinitely
n (person)	**verb forms**	**adv**	**other**
x	x	x	x

<u>Collocations from the ACL</u>
adj+n: finite number, infinite number.

foundation

[faʊndeɪʃən]

noun

1. the basis on which something is grounded. E.g.: **there is little foundation for his objections**
2. an institution supported by an endowment.
3. education or instruction in the fundamentals of a field of knowledge. E.g.: **he lacks the foundation necessary for advanced study** [Syn: *grounding*]
4. the fundamental assumptions from which something is begun or developed or calculated or explained. [Syn: *basis, base, fundament, groundwork, cornerstone*]
5. lowest support of a structure. [Syn: *base, fundament, foot, groundwork, substructure, understructure*]

n (thing)	**verb**	**adj**	**opposite**
foundation	x	x	x
n (person)	**verb forms**	**adv**	**other**
x	x	x	x

---

globe

[gloʊb]

noun

1. an object with a spherical shape. [Syn: *ball, orb*]
2. the 3rd planet from the sun; the planet on which we live. [Syn: *Earth, world*]
3. a sphere on which a map (especially of the earth) is represented.

n (thing)	**verb**	**adj**	**opposite**
globalisation globalization globe	x	global	x
n (person)	**verb forms**	**adv**	**other**
x	x	globally	x

<u>Collocations from the ACL</u>

adj+n: global capitalism, global context, global culture, global economy, global issue, global market, global marketplace, global media, global network, global perspective, global shift, global structure, global trade, global village.

grade

[greɪd]

verb

1. assign a grade or rank to, according to one's evaluation. E.g.: **grade tests** [Syn: *score, mark*]
2. assign a rank or rating to. [Syn: *rate, rank, range, order, place*]

noun

1. a relative position or degree of value in a graded group. E.g.: **lumber of the highest grade** [Syn: *level, tier*]
2. a body of students who are taught together. [Syn: *class, form*]
3. a number or letter indicating quality (especially of a student's performance). E.g.: **grade A milk** [Syn: *mark, score*]

n (thing)	**verb**	**adj**	**opposite**
grade	grade	graded	x
n (person)	**verb forms**	**adv**	**other**
x	graded grades grading	x	x

guarantee

[gerənti]

verb

1. promise to do or accomplish. E.g.: **guarantee to free the prisoners** [Syn: *undertake*]
2. make certain of. E.g.: **Preparation will guarantee success!** [Syn: *ensure*, *insure*, *assure*, *secure*]

noun

1. a written assurance that some product or service will be provided or will meet certain specifications. [Syn: *warrant*, *warrantee*, *warranty*]
2. a pledge that something will happen or that something is true. E.g.: **there is no guarantee that they are not lying**

n (thing)	**verb**	**adj**	**opposite**
guarantee	guarantee	guaranteed	x
n (person)	**verb forms**	**adv**	**other**
x	guaranteed guaranteeing guarantees	x	x

hierarchy

[haɪ ɜrɑrki]

noun

1. the organization of people at different ranks in an administrative body. [Syn: *power structure, pecking order*]
2. a series of ordered groupings of people or things within a system. E.g.: **put honesty first in her hierarchy of values**

n (thing)	**verb**	**adj**	**opposite**
hierarchy	x	hierarchical	x
n (person)	**verb forms**	**adv**	**other**
x	x	x	x

----

identical

[aɪ dent ɪ kəl]

adj

1. exactly alike; incapable of being perceived as different. E.g.: **rows of identical houses, cars identical except for their license plates** [Syn: *indistinguishable*]
2. (of twins) derived from a single egg or ovum. E.g.: **identical twins are monovular** [Syn: *monovular*]

n (thing)	**verb**	**adj**	**opposite**
x	x	identical	x
n (person)	**verb forms**	**adv**	**other**
x	x	identically	x

ideology

[aɪdiɑlədʒi]

noun

1. an orientation that characterizes the thinking of a group or nation. [Syn: *political orientation, political theory*]

n (thing)	**verb**	**adj**	**opposite**
ideology	x	ideological	x
n (person)	**verb forms**	**adv**	**other**
x	x	ideologically	x

Collocations from the ACL

adj+n: dominant ideology, political ideology.

---

infer

[ɪnfɜr]

verb

1. reason by deduction; establish by deduction. [Syn: *deduce, deduct, derive*]
2. draw from specific cases for more general cases. [Syn: *generalize, generalise, extrapolate*]

n (thing)	**verb**	**adj**	**opposite**
inference	infer	x	x
n (person)	**verb forms**	**adv**	**other**
x	inferred inferring infers	x	x

innovate

[ɪnəveɪt]

verb

1. bring something new to an environment. [Syn: *introduce*]

n (thing)	verb	adj	opposite
innovation	innovate	innovative	x
n (person)	**verb forms**	**adv**	**other**
innovator	innovated innovates innovating	x	x

----

insert

[ɪnsɜrt]

verb

1. put or introduce into something. E.g.: **insert a picture into the text** [Syn: *infix*, *enter*, *introduce*]

noun

1. an artifact that is inserted or is to be inserted. [Syn: *inset*]

n (thing)	verb	adj	opposite
insert insertion	insert	x	x
n (person)	**verb forms**	**adv**	**other**
x	inserted inserting inserts	x	x

intervene

[ɪnt3rvin]

verb

1. get involved, so as to alter or hinder an action, or through force or threat of force. E.g.: **Why did the U.S. not intervene earlier in WW II?** [Syn: *step in, interfere, interpose*]
2. occur between other event or between certain points of time. E.g.: **the war intervened between the birth of her two children**

n (thing)	verb	adj	opposite
intervention	intervene	intervening	x
n (person)	**verb forms**	**adv**	**other**
x	intervened intervenes intervening	x	x

---

isolate

[aɪsəleɪt]

verb

1. place or set apart. E.g.: **They isolated the political prisoners from the other inmates** [Syn: *insulate*]
2. obtain in pure form. E.g.: **The chemist managed to isolate the compound**

n (thing)	verb	adj	opposite
isolation isolationism	isolate	isolated	x
n (person)	**verb forms**	**adv**	**other**
x	isolated isolates isolating	x	x

media

[midiə]

noun

1. the internet, newspapers, magazines, television, and other means of communication that reach and influence people widely (usually used with plural verb).
2. plural of medium.

n (thing)	verb	adj	opposite
media	x	x	x
n (person)	**verb forms**	**adv**	**other**
x	x	x	x

Collocations from the ACL

adj+n: digital media, electronic media, global media, national media, popular media, visual media.

---

mode

[moʊd]

noun

1. a particular functioning condition or arrangement. E.g.: **switched from keyboard to voice mode**
2. the most frequent value of a random variable. [Syn: *modal value*]
3. how something is done or how it happens. E.g.: **their nomadic mode of existence** [Syn: *manner, style, way, fashion*]

n (thing)	verb	adj	opposite
mode	x	x	x
n (person)	**verb forms**	**adv**	**other**
x	x	x	x

paradigm

[perədaɪm]

noun

1. a standard or typical example. [Syn: *prototype*, *epitome*, *image*]
2. the generally accepted perspective of a particular discipline at a given time. E.g.: **he framed the problem within the psychoanalytic paradigm**

n (thing)	**verb**	**adj**	**opposite**
paradigm	x	x	x
n (person)	**verb forms**	**adv**	**other**
x	x	x	x

----

phenomenon

[fənɑmənɑn]

noun

1. a remarkable development.
2. any state or process known through the senses rather than by intuition or reasoning.

n (thing)	**verb**	**adj**	**opposite**
phenomenon	x	phenomenal	x
n (person)	**verb forms**	**adv**	**other**
x	x	x	phenomena (pl)

Collocations from the ACL

adj+n: cultural phenomenon, social phenomenon.

priority

[praɪɔrəti]

noun

1. status established in order of importance or urgency. E.g.: **national independence takes priority over class struggle** [Syn: *precedence, precedency*]

n (thing)	verb	adj	opposite
prioritisation prioritization priority	prioritise prioritize	x	x
n (person)	**verb forms**	**adv**	**other**
x	prioritised / -ized prioritises / -izes prioritising / -izing	x	x

Collocations from the ACL
adj+n: first priority, high priority, low priority.

---

prohibit

[proʊhɪbət]

verb

1. command against. [Syn: *forbid, interdict, proscribe, veto, disallow*]

n (thing)	verb	adj	opposite
prohibition	prohibit	prohibited prohibitive	x
n (person)	**verb forms**	**adv**	**other**
x	prohibited prohibiting prohibits	x	x

publication

[pʌblɪkeɪʃən]

noun

1. a copy of a printed work offered for distribution.
2. the act of issuing printed materials. [Syn: *issue*]

n (thing)	verb	adj	opposite
publication	x	x	x
n (person)	**verb forms**	**adv**	**other**
x	x	x	x

---

quote

[kwoʊt]

verb

1. put quote marks around.
2. repeat a passage from. E.g.: **He quoted the Bible to her** [Syn: *cite*]

noun

1. a passage or expression that is quoted or cited. [Syn: *quotation, citation*]
2. a punctuation mark used to attribute the enclosed text to someone else. [Syn: *quotation mark, inverted comma*]

n (thing)	verb	adj	opposite
quotation quote	quote	x	x
n (person)	**verb forms**	**adv**	**other**
x	quoted quotes quoting	x	x

release

[rilis]

verb

1. grant freedom to; free from confinement. [Syn: *free, liberate, unloose, unloosen, loose*]
2. make (information) available publication. E.g.: **release the list with the names of the prisoners** [Syn: *free*]
3. release, as from one's grip. [Syn: *let go of, let go, relinquish*]

noun

1. a process that liberates or discharges something. E.g.: **there was a sudden release of oxygen, the release of iodine from the thyroid gland**
2. the act of liberating someone or something. [Syn: *liberation, freeing*]
3. the act of allowing a fluid to escape. [Syn: *spill, spillage*]

n (thing)	**verb**	**adj**	**opposite**
release	release	x	x
n (person)	**verb forms**	**adv**	**other**
x	released releases releasing	x	x

reverse

[rɪv3rs]

adj

1. reversed (turned backward) in order or nature or effect. [Syn: *inverse*]

verb

1. turn inside out or upside down. [Syn: *invert*]
2. change to the contrary. E.g.: **The trend was reversed** [Syn: *change by reversal, turn*]

noun

1. a relation of direct opposition. E.g.: **we thought Sue was older than Bill but just the reverse was true** [Syn: *contrary, opposite*]

n (thing)	verb	adj	opposite
reversal reverse	reverse	reverse reversible	irreversible
n (person)	**verb forms**	**adv**	**other**
x	reversed reverses reversing	x	x

simulate

[sɪmjələt]

verb

1. make a pretence of. [Syn: *assume, sham, feign*]
2. create a representation or model of. [Syn: *model*]
3. reproduce someone's behavior or looks. [Syn: *imitate, copy*]

n (thing)	**verb**	**adj**	**opposite**
simulation	simulate	simulated	x
n (person)	**verb forms**	**adv**	**other**
x	simulated simulates simulating	x	x

---

sole

[soʊl]

adj

1. not divided or shared with others. E.g.: **sole rights of publication** [Syn: *exclusive*]
2. being the only one; single and isolated from others. E.g.: **the sole heir**, **the sole example** [Syn: *solitary, only, lonesome, lone*]

n (thing)	**verb**	**adj**	**opposite**
x	x	sole	x
n (person)	**verb forms**	**adv**	**other**
x	x	solely	x

somewhat

[sʌmwʌt]

adv

1. to a moderately sufficient extent or degree. [Syn: *reasonably*, *moderately*, *within reason*, *fairly*, *middling*, *passably*]
2. to a small degree or extent. E.g.: **his arguments were somewhat self-contradictory** [Syn: *slightly*]

n (thing)	verb	adj	opposite
x	x	x	x
n (person)	**verb forms**	**adv**	**other**
x	x	somewhat	x

---

submit

[səbmɪt]

verb

1. hand over formally. [Syn: *present*]
2. yield to the control of another.
3. make an application as for a job or funding. [Syn: *put in*]

n (thing)	verb	adj	opposite
submission	submit	x	x
n (person)	**verb forms**	**adv**	**other**
x	submits submitted submitting	x	x

successor

[səksesɜr]

noun

1. a person who inherits some title or office. [Syn: *heir*]
2. a person who follows next in order. E.g.: **he was President Lincoln's successor** [Syn: *replacement*]

n (thing)	verb	adj	opposite
succession	x	successive	x
n (person)	**verb forms**	**adv**	**other**
successor	x	successively	x

---

survive

[sɜrvaɪv]

verb

1. continue to live; endure or last. E.g.: **These superstitions survive in the backwaters of America** [Syn: *last, live, live on, go, endure, hold up, hold out*]

n (thing)	verb	adj	opposite
survival	survive	x	x
n (person)	**verb forms**	**adv**	**other**
survivor	survived survives surviving	x	x

thesis

[θisɪs]

noun

1. a treatise advancing a new point of view resulting from research; usually a requirement for an advanced academic degree. [Syn: *dissertation*]
2. an unproved statement put forward as a premise in an argument.

n (thing)	verb	adj	opposite
thesis	x	x	x
n (person)	**verb forms**	**adv**	**other**
x	x	x	theses (pl)

---

topic

[tapɪk]

noun

1. the subject matter of a conversation or discussion. E.g.: **it was a very sensitive topic** [Syn: *subject, theme*]
2. some situation or event that is thought about. E.g.: **he kept drifting off the topic** [Syn: *subject, issue, matter*]

n (thing)	verb	adj	opposite
topic	x	topical	x
n (person)	**verb forms**	**adv**	**other**
x	x	x	x

Collocations from the ACL

adj+n: key topic, related topic.

v+n: cover (a) topic, discuss (a) topic.

transmit

[trænzmɪt]

verb

1. send from one person or place to another. E.g.: **transmit a message** [Syn: *transfer, transport, channel, channelize, channelise*]
2. broadcast over the airwaves, as in radio or television. [Syn: *air, send, broadcast, beam*]

n (thing)	verb	adj	opposite
transmission	transmit	x	x
n (person)	**verb forms**	**adv**	**other**
x	transmits transmitted transmitting	x	x

Collocations from the ACL

v+n: transmit data, transmit information.

---

ultimate

[ʌltəmət]

adj

1. furthest or highest in degree or order; utmost or extreme. E.g.: **the ultimate achievement, the ultimate question, man's ultimate destiny, the ultimate insult, one's ultimate goal in life**
2. being the last or concluding element of a series. E.g.: **the ultimate sonata of that opus, a distinction between the verb and noun senses of `conflict' is that in the verb the stress is on the ultimate (or last) syllable**

n (thing)	verb	adj	opposite
x	x	ultimate	x
n (person)	**verb forms**	**adv**	**other**
x	x	ultimately	x

unique

[junik]

adj

1. the single one of its kind. E.g.: **the unique existing example of Donne's handwriting, a unique copy of an ancient manuscript, certain types of problems have unique solutions** [Syn: *singular*]
2. (followed by `to') applying exclusively to a given category or condition or locality. E.g.: **a species unique to Australia**
3. highly unusual or rare but not the single instance. E.g.: **spoke with a unique accent, had unique ability in raising funds, a frankness unique in literature, a unique dining experience**

n (thing)	**verb**	**adj**	**opposite**
uniqueness	x	unique	x
n (person)	**verb forms**	**adv**	**other**
x	x	uniquely	x

<u>Collocations from the ACL</u>

adj+n: unique individual, unique opportunity, unique position.

visible

[vɪzəbəl]

adj

1. perceptible especially by the eye; or open to easy view. E.g.: **a visible object, visible stars, mountains visible in the distance, a visible change of expression, visible files** [Syn: *seeable*]

n (thing)	**verb**	**adj**	**opposite**
visibility	x	visible	invisibility invisible
n (person)	**verb forms**	**adv**	**other**
x	x	visibly	x

Collocations from the ACL
v+adj: become visible, make visible.

----

voluntary

[vɑlənteri]

adj

1. of your own free will or design; not forced or compelled. E.g.: **man is a voluntary agent, participation was voluntary, voluntary manslaughter, voluntary generosity in times of disaster, voluntary social workers, a voluntary confession**

n (thing)	**verb**	**adj**	**opposite**
x	volunteer	voluntary	x
n (person)	**verb forms**	**adv**	**other**
volunteer	volunteered volunteering volunteers	voluntarily	x

Exercises (Sublist 7)

Task 1: Focus on Meaning #1

Study the following text on **Sources of Energy**. Fill in the gaps using words from the box. All are words from AWL sublist 7. [Note: words from sublist 8 (*italics*), sublist 9 (**bold**) and sublist 10 (***italics+bold***) are also shown, for preview purposes.]

chemical	comprised	conversion	converted	converts
decades	disposal	extracted	finite	global
infinite	release	released	visible	

Energy is an important element at all levels of society. We live in a very interdependent world, and access to adequate and reliable energy resources is *crucial* for economic growth and for maintaining the quality of our lives. There are two major types of energy sources: renewable and non-renewable. Renewable sources are energy sources that are replenished through naturally occurring, **ongoing** processes, on a time scale that is much shorter than the **anticipated** lifetime of the civilization using the source, making them almost _____________. Non-renewable sources are depleted once some of the energy they contain is _____________ and transformed into other kinds of energy, which means they are _____________. The natural processes by which non-renewable sources are formed typically take place over geological time scales.

Our most important non-renewable energy sources are fossil fuels, such as coal, petroleum, and natural gas. These account for 81% of the world's energy consumption. Burning fossil fuels creates _____________ reactions that transform potential energy, in the molecular structures of the reactants, into thermal energy and products. This thermal energy can be used to heat buildings or to operate steam-driven machinery. Electrical power generation is mostly derived from transferring energy in expanding steam, *via* turbines, into mechanical work, which rotates coils of wire in magnetic fields to generate electricity.

Nuclear energy is the other non-renewable source and supplies about 3% of the world's consumption. *Nuclear* reactions generate energy by transforming potential energy, in the structure of nuclei, into thermal energy. The thermal energy obtained from *nuclear* reactions can be transferred into other forms in the same ways that energy from fossil fuels are used.

An unfortunate byproduct of relying on energy produced from the combustion of fossil fuels is the _____________ of carbon dioxide into the atmosphere and its contribution to _____________ warming. *Nuclear* energy ***poses*** environmental problems as well, including the safety and _____________ of *nuclear* waste. Besides these important consequences, reserves of non-renewable sources of energy are limited and, given the rapidly growing rate of world energy consumption, may not last for more than a few hundred years. Some estimate that oil reserves will be exhausted within mere _____________.

Four renewable energy sources which involve quite different types of energy transformations from those just discussed are hydropower, wind power, geothermal power, and solar power.

Hydropower is produced by the _____________ of the gravitational potential energy of falling or flowing water into kinetic energy and then into work to run electric generators or machinery. Wats to harness the mechanical energy in ocean surface waves and tides is in development.

Wind power also _____________ kinetic energy into work, which can be used directly to generate electricity, operate mills, and propel sailboats.

The interior of Earth has a great deal of thermal energy, part of which is left over from its original formation and part of which is _____________ from radioactive minerals (a form of natural *nuclear* energy). It will take a very long time for this geothermal energy to escape into space, so people generally regard it as a renewable source, when actually, it is just inexhaustible on human time scales.

The source of solar power is energy carried by the electromagnetic waves radiated by the Sun. Most of this energy is carried by _____________ light and infrared (heat) radiation. When suitable materials absorb electromagnetic waves, radiant energy is _____________ into thermal energy, which can be used to heat water, or when concentrated, to make steam and generate electricity. However, another way to generate energy from sunlight is *via* photovoltaics (PV), which are _____________ of semi-conductor materials such as silicon which produce electricity directly using what is known as the photoelectric effect.

Source: Adapted from University Physics, Volume 1, in Chapter 8 | Potential Energy and Conservation of Energy © 2017 Rice University. Download for free at https://openstax.org/details/books/university-physics-volume-1.

Task 2: Focus on Meaning #2

Read the following text on **Classification of Matter**. Fill in the gaps using words from the box. All are from AWL sublist 7. [Note: words from sublist 8 (*italics*), sublist 9 (**bold**) and sublist 10 (***italics+bold***) are again shown.]

comprehensive	definite	differentiate	identical
phenomenon	somewhat	unique	

Matter is defined as anything that occupies space and has mass, and it is all around us. Solids and liquids are more obviously matter: We can see that they take up space, and their weight tells us that they have mass. Gases are also matter; if gases did not take up space, a balloon would not inflate (increase its volume) when filled with gas.

Solids, liquids, and gases are the three states of matter commonly found on earth. A solid is **rigid** and possesses a _____________ shape. A liquid flows and takes the shape of its container, except that it forms a flat or slightly curved upper surface when acted upon by gravity, a _____________ which does not happen in space (in zero gravity, liquids assume a **spherical** shape). Both liquid and solid samples have volumes that are very nearly independent of pressure. A gas takes both the shape and volume of its container.

A _____________ classification of matter should include a fourth state, plasma, which occurs naturally in the interiors of stars. A plasma is a gaseous state of matter that contains *appreciable* numbers of electrically charged particles. The presence of these charged particles imparts ___________ properties to plasmas that ___________ them from gases and justify their classification as a distinct state of matter. In addition to stars, plasmas are found in some other high-temperature environments, both natural and man-made, such as lightning strikes and certain television screens.

Some samples of matter appear to have properties of solids, liquids, and/or gases at the same time. This can occur when the sample is composed of many small pieces, for example sand, which can be poured in an _____________ way to how a liquid is poured because it is composed of many small grains of solid sand. Matter can also have properties of more than one state when it is a mixture, such as with clouds. Clouds appear to behave _____________ like gases, though they are actually mixtures of air (gas) and tiny particles of water (liquid or solid).

Source: Adapted from University Chemistry 2e, in Chapter 1 | Essential Ideas © 2017 Rice University. Download for free at https://openstax.org/details/books/chemistry-2e.

Task 3: Focus on Meaning #3

The following sentences each contain an underlined word, which can be replaced by a synonym from the box below (synonyms in the box are all sublist 7 words). Replace each word with the correct synonym. An example has been done.

contrary	coupled	~~dispose~~	filed	foundation
grades	guarantee	mode	paradigms	publication
solely	thesis	ultimately		

Example: Great care needs to be taken by technicians in nuclear power plants when they ***get rid*** *of nuclear waste.* __*dispose*__

a) Although each half of the brain is associated with certain functions, both areas interact to provide the **basis** for our thoughts and behaviours. ________________

b) Military expenditure, **combined** with a decrease in tax revenue, have been the main contributors to the growing budget deficit. ________________

c) In Douglas McGregor's classification, Theory X managers believe that people are **only** motivated by money. ________________

d) Access to financial capital helps a business to make physical capital investments, and, **in the end**, can lead to job creation. ________________

e) A peer-reviewed journal article is read by several other experts in the same field to provide feedback about the quality of the article before it is accepted for **printing**. ________________

f) Beliefs about racial differences and performance levels of athletes persist despite a number of examples to the **opposite**. ________________

g) The informed consent form will provide participants with a **certainty** that any data collected in the experiment will remain confidential. ________________

h) Scholars in each of the three major **perspectives** of sociology would view the topic in a different way. ________________

i) The primary **means** of communication for deaf people is sign language. ________________

j) It took a long time to find the book in the library as it had been **placed** in the Child Psychology section rather than in the Adult Psychology section. ________________

k) Lack of parental discipline can be associated with lower **scores** in school. ________________

l) The teacher disagreed with his **viewpoint** that all people are lazy. ______________

Task 4: Collocations #1

Match the following words to form common collocations of AWL sublist 7 words. An example has been done for you.

become	example
infinite	data
classic	decades
recent	ideology
high	visible
cultural	priority
transmit	number
political	phenomenon

Task 5: Collocations #2

The following collocations match *one* word from the AWL sublist 7. Identify which one. Choose from the following words.

comprehensive	decade(s)	dynamic
empirical	extract	global
media	topic	unique

key --, related --, cover (a) --, discuss (a) --	
-- individual, -- opportunity, -- position	
digital --, electronic --, global --, national --, popular --, visual --	
-- account, -- approach, -- overview, -- review, -- system	
next --, previous --, early --, recent --.	
-- capitalism, -- context, -- culture, -- economy, -- issue, -- market, -- marketplace, -- media, -- network, -- perspective, -- shift, -- structure, -- trade, -- village	
-- equilibrium, -- nature, -- process, -- system	
-- data, -- information	
-- data, -- evidence, -- investigation, -- research, -- study, -- support, -- work	

Task 6: Word form #1

Complete the following sentences by changing the word form of the word(s) in brackets. An example has been done for you.

Example: There are many economic (economy) benefits of the policy.

a) There were many ______________ (voluntary) who assisted the hospital during the Covid-19 crisis.
b) His qualities as a great leader were ______________ (deny). There was no one who disagreed.
c) The reckless action of the president was halted by the ______________ (intervene) of his chief of staff.
d) The psychological problems which children suffer from will often persist into ______________ (adult).
e) Scientists are working on increasingly ______________ (innovate) solutions to the energy crisis.
f) Most adults are more interested in intimacy than in ______________ (isolate) from others.
g) The cost of the treatment was ______________ (prohibit), which led to the company discontinuing its research in the area.
h) The company operated on a very ______________ (hierarchy) system, and employees could not communicate above their immediate supervisor.
i) Many believe that the sacrifice made by Coretta Scott King, Martin Luther King's wife, ______________ (aid) his success.
j) The company ______________ (channel) most information for the public through its official website.
k) Some psychologists employ virtual reality therapy to give patients a ______________ (simulate) and so help them overcome their fears.
l) It is important to use ______________ (quote) marks, along with an in-text citation, when copying someone's exact words into your text.

Task 7: Word form #2

Change the following v/adj forms to make the noun 'thing' form. An example has been done. Note: have more than one noun form.

adapt ________________ / ________________
advocate ________________
confirm ________________
convert ________________
deny *denial*
dispose ________________
eliminate ________________
equip ________________
extract ________________ / ________________
infer ________________
innovate ________________
insert ________________ / ________________
prioritise ________________ / ________________
quote ________________ / ________________
reverse ________________ / ________________
submit ________________
successor ________________
survive ________________
transmit ________________
unique ________________
visible ________________

Then, put these noun forms in the correct column of the table below.

-al	**-ance/ -ence**	**-cy**	**-bility**	**-ment**	**-rsion**	***Same as v/adj form***
denial						
			-ity	**-ness**	**-ssion**	**-tion**

Academic Word List:

Sublist 8

abandon

[əbændən]

verb

1. forsake, leave behind. E.g.: **We abandoned the old car in the empty parking lot**
2. stop maintaining or insisting on; of ideas, claims, etc. E.g.: **He abandoned the thought of asking for her hand in marriage** [Syn: *give up*]

n (thing)	**verb**	**adj**	**opposite**
abandonment	abandon	x	x
n (person)	**verb forms**	**adv**	**other**
x	abandoned abandoning abandons	x	x

---

accompany

[əkʌmpəni]

verb

1. be associated with. [Syn: *attach to, come with, go with*]
2. be a companion to somebody. [Syn: *company, companion, keep company*]

n (thing)	**verb**	**adj**	**opposite**
accompaniment	accompany	x	unaccompanied
n (person)	**verb forms**	**adv**	**other**
x	accompanied accompanies accompanying	x	x

accumulate

[əkjumjəleɪt]

verb

1. collect or gather. [Syn: *cumulate, conglomerate, pile up, gather, amass*]

n (thing)	**verb**	**adj**	**opposite**
accumulation	accumulate	x	x
n (person)	**verb forms**	**adv**	**other**
x	accumulated accumulates accumulating	x	x

----

ambiguous

[æmbɪgjuəs]

adj

1. open to two or more interpretations; or of uncertain nature or significance; or (often) intended to mislead. E.g.: **the polling had a complex and equivocal (or ambiguous) message for potential female candidates** [Syn: *equivocal*]

n (thing)	**verb**	**adj**	**opposite**
ambiguity	x	ambiguous	unambiguous unambiguously
n (person)	**verb forms**	**adv**	**other**
x	x	x	x

append

[əpend]

verb

1. fix to; attach. E.g.: **append a charm to the necklace** [Syn: *tag on*, *tack on*, *tack*, *hang on*]
2. add to the very end. E.g.: **He appended a glossary to his novel where he used an invented language** [Syn: *add on*, *supplement*, *affix*]

n (thing)	verb	adj	opposite
appendix	append	x	x
n (person)	**verb forms**	**adv**	**other**
x	appended appending appends	x	appendices (pl) appendixes (pl)

---

appreciate

[əpriʃieɪt]

verb

1. recognize with gratitude; be grateful for.
2. gain in value. E.g.: **The yen appreciated again!** [Syn: *apprize*, *apprise*, *revalue*]
3. be fully aware of; realize fully. E.g.: **Do you appreciate the full meaning of this letter?** [Syn: *take account*]

n (thing)	verb	adj	opposite
appreciation	appreciate	appreciable	unappreciated
n (person)	**verb forms**	**adv**	**other**
x	appreciated appreciates appreciating	appreciably	x

arbitrary

[ɑrbətreri]

adj

1. based on or subject to individual discretion or preference or sometimes impulse or caprice. E.g.: **an arbitrary decision, the arbitrary rule of a dictator, an arbitrary penalty, of arbitrary size and shape, an arbitrary choice, arbitrary division of t**

n (thing)	verb	adj	opposite
arbitrariness	x	arbitrary	x
n (person)	**verb forms**	**adv**	**other**
x	x	arbitrarily	x

----

automate

[ɔtəmeɪt]

verb

1. make automatic or control or operate automatically. E.g.: **automate the movement of the robot** [Syn: *automatize, automatise*]

n (thing)	verb	adj	opposite
automation	automate	automated automatic	x
n (person)	**verb forms**	**adv**	**other**
x	automated automates automating	automatically	x

bias

[baɪəs]

verb

1. influence in an unfair way. E.g.: **you are biasing my choice by telling me yours**

noun

1. a partiality that prevents objective consideration of an issue or situation. [Syn: *prejudice, preconception*]

n (thing)	**verb**	**adj**	**opposite**
bias	bias	biased	unbiased
n (person)	**verb forms**	**adv**	**other**
x	biased biases biasing	x	x

---

chart

[tʃart]

verb

1. represent by means of a graph. E.g.: **chart the data** [Syn: *graph*]
2. plan in detail. E.g.: **The president is charting a course out of recession**

noun

1. a visual display of information.

n (thing)	**verb**	**adj**	**opposite**
chart	chart	x	uncharted
n (person)	**verb forms**	**adv**	**other**
x	charted charting charts	x	x

clarify

[klerəfaɪ]

verb

1. make clear and (more) comprehensible. E.g.: **clarify the mystery surrounding her death** [Syn: *clear up, elucidate*]

n (thing)	**verb**	**adj**	**opposite**
clarification clarity	clarify	x	x
n (person)	**verb forms**	**adv**	**other**
x	clarified clarifies clarifying	x	x

----

commodity

[kəmɑdəti]

noun

1. articles of commerce. [Syn: *trade goods, goods*]

n (thing)	**verb**	**adj**	**opposite**
commodity	x	x	x
n (person)	**verb forms**	**adv**	**other**
x	x	x	x

complement

[kɑmpləmənt]

verb

1. make complete or perfect; supply what is wanting or form the complement to. E.g.: **I need some pepper to complement the sweet touch in the soup**

noun

1. something added to complete or make perfect. E.g.: **a fine wine is a perfect complement to the dinner**
2. either of two parts that mutually complete each other.

n (thing)	**verb**	**adj**	**opposite**
complement	complement	complementary	x
n (person)	**verb forms**	**adv**	**other**
x	complemented complementing complements	x	x

---

conform

[kənfɔrm]

verb

1. be similar, be in line with.
2. adapt or conform oneself to new or different conditions. [Syn: *adjust*, *adapt*]

n (thing)	**verb**	**adj**	**opposite**
conformability conformance conformation conformity	conform	conformable conformist	non-conformist non-conformity nonconformist nonconformity
n (person)	**verb forms**	**adv**	**other**
conformist	conformed conforming conforms	x	x

contemporary

[kəntempɜreri]

adj

1. occurring in the same period of time. E.g.: **the composer Salieri was contemporary with Mozart** [Syn: *contemporaneous*]
2. belonging to the present time. E.g.: **contemporary leaders** [Syn: *present-day*]

noun

1. a person of nearly the same age as another. [Syn: *coeval*]

n (thing)	**verb**	**adj**	**opposite**
x	x	contemporary	x
n (person)	**verb forms**	**adv**	**other**
contemporary	x	x	x

<u>Collocations from the ACL</u>

adj+n: contemporary debate, contemporary issue, contemporary life, contemporary society, contemporary world.

----

contradict

[kɑntrədɪkt]

verb

1. prove negative; show to be false. [Syn: *negate*]

n (thing)	**verb**	**adj**	**opposite**
contradiction	contradict	contradictory	x
n (person)	**verb forms**	**adv**	**other**
x	contradicted contradicting contradicts	x	x

crucial

[kruʃəl]

adj

1. of extreme importance; vital to the resolution of a crisis. E.g.: **a crucial moment in his career**, **a crucial election**, **a crucial issue for women** [Syn: *important*]
2. having the power or quality of deciding. E.g.: **the crucial experiment** [Syn: *determining*, *deciding*, *determinant*, *determinative*]

n (thing)	**verb**	**adj**	**opposite**
x	x	crucial	x
n (person)	**verb forms**	**adv**	**other**
x	x	crucially	x

Collocations from the ACL

adj+n: crucial difference, crucial factor, crucial importance, crucial part, crucial point, crucial question, crucial role.

---

currency

[kɜrənsi]

noun

1. a current state of general acceptance and use. [Syn: *vogue*]
2. the metal or paper medium of exchange that is presently used.

n (thing)	**verb**	**adj**	**opposite**
currency	x	x	x
n (person)	**verb forms**	**adv**	**other**
x	x	x	x

Collocations from the ACL

adj+n: foreign currency, single currency.

denote

[dɪnoʊt]

verb

1. have as a meaning. E.g.: **`multi-' denotes `many'** [Syn: *refer*]

n (thing)	verb	adj	opposite
denotation	denote	x	x
n (person)	**verb forms**	**adv**	**other**
x	denoted denotes denoting	x	x

---

detect

[dɪtekt]

verb

1. discover or determine the existence, presence, or fact of. E.g.: **She detected high levels of lead in her drinking water** [Syn: *observe, find, discover, notice*]

n (thing)	verb	adj	opposite
detection detector	detect	detectable	x
n (person)	**verb forms**	**adv**	**other**
detective	detected detecting detects	x	x

deviate

[divieɪt]

verb

1. turn aside; turn away from. [Syn: *divert*]
2. be at variance with; be out of line with. [Syn: *vary*, *diverge*, *depart*]

n (thing)	verb	adj	opposite
deviation	deviate	x	x
n (person)	**verb forms**	**adv**	**other**
x	deviated deviates deviating	x	x

---

displace

[dɪspleɪs]

verb

1. move (people) forcibly from their homeland into a new and foreign environment. [Syn: *uproot*, *deracinate*]
2. put out of its usual place, position, or relationship. E.g.: **The colonists displaced the natives** [Syn: *dislocate*]

n (thing)	verb	adj	opposite
displacement	displace	x	x
n (person)	**verb forms**	**adv**	**other**
x	displaced displaces displacing	x	x

drama

[drɑmə]

noun

1. a dramatic work intended for performance by actors on a stage. [Syn: *play*, *dramatic play*]
2. an episode that is turbulent or highly emotional. [Syn: *dramatic event*]

n (thing)	**verb**	**adj**	**opposite**
drama dramatisation dramatization	dramatise dramatize	dramatic	x
n (person)	**verb forms**	**adv**	**other**
dramatist	dramatised / -ized dramatises / -izes dramatizing / -izing	dramatically	x

<u>Collocations from the ACL</u>
adj+n: dramatic change, dramatic effect, dramatic increase.
v+adv: change dramatically, increase dramatically.

---

eventual

[əventʃuəl]

adj

1. expected to follow in the indefinite future from causes already operating. E.g.: **hope of eventual (or ultimate) rescue, if this trend continues it is not reasonable to expect the eventual collapse of the stock market**

n (thing)	**verb**	**adj**	**opposite**
eventuality	x	eventual	x
n (person)	**verb forms**	**adv**	**other**
x	x	eventually	x

exhibit

[ɪgzɪbɪt]

verb

1. to show, make visible or apparent. E.g.: **The Metropolitan Museum is exhibiting Goya's works this month** [Syn: *expose*, *display*]

n (thing)	verb	adj	opposite
exhibition	exhibit	x	x
n (person)	**verb forms**	**adv**	**other**
x	exhibited exhibiting exhibits	x	x

----

exploit

[eksplɔɪt]

verb

1. use or manipulate to one's advantage. E.g.: **He exploited the new taxation system** [Syn: *work*]

n (thing)	verb	adj	opposite
exploitation	exploit	exploited	x
n (person)	**verb forms**	**adv**	**other**
x	exploited exploiting exploits	x	x

Collocations from the ACL

adj+n: economic exploitation, sexual exploitation.

fluctuate

[flʌktʃəweɪt]

verb

1. be unstable; have ups and downs. E.g.: **The stock market fluctuates**

n (thing)	verb	adj	opposite
fluctuation	fluctuate	fluctuating	x
n (person)	**verb forms**	**adv**	**other**
x	fluctuated fluctuates fluctuating	x	x

---

guideline

[gaɪdlaɪn]

noun

1. a rule or principle that provides guidance to appropriate behavior. [Syn: *guidepost, rule of thumb*]

n (thing)	verb	adj	opposite
guideline	x	x	x
n (person)	**verb forms**	**adv**	**other**
x	x	x	x

highlight

[haɪlaɪt]

verb

1. move into the foreground to make more visible or prominent. E.g.: **The introduction highlighted the speaker's distinguished career in linguistics** [Syn: *foreground, spotlight, play up*]

noun

1. the most interesting or memorable part. E.g.: **the highlight of the tour was our visit to the Vatican** [Syn: *high spot*]

n (thing)	verb	adj	opposite
highlight	highlight	x	x
n (person)	**verb forms**	**adv**	**other**
x	highlighted highlighting highlights	x	x

----

implicit

[ɪmplɪsət]

adj

1. implied though not directly expressed; inherent in the nature of something. E.g.: **an implicit agreement not to raise the subject, there was implicit criticism in his voice, anger was implicit in the argument, the oak is implicit in the acorn** [Syn: *inexplicit*]

n (thing)	verb	adj	opposite
x	x	implicit	x
n (person)	**verb forms**	**adv**	**other**
x	x	implicitly	x

induce

[ɪndus]

verb

1. cause to arise. E.g.: **induce a crisis** [Syn: *bring on*]
2. reason or establish by induction.

n (thing)	**verb**	**adj**	**opposite**
induction	induce	x	x
n (person)	**verb forms**	**adv**	**other**
x	induced induces inducing	x	x

---

inevitable

[ɪnevətəbəl]

adj

1. incapable of being avoided or prevented. E.g.: **the inevitable result**

noun

1. an unavoidable event. E.g.: **don't argue with the inevitable**

n (thing)	**verb**	**adj**	**opposite**
inevitability inevitable	x	inevitable	x
n (person)	**verb forms**	**adv**	**other**
x	x	inevitably	x

infrastructure

[ɪnfrəstrʌktʃɜr]

noun

1. the stock of basic facilities and capital equipment needed for the functioning of a country or area. [Syn: *base*]
2. the basic structure or features of a system or organization. [Syn: *substructure*]

n (thing)	verb	adj	opposite
infrastructure	x	x	x
n (person)	**verb forms**	**adv**	**other**
x	x	x	x

----

inspect

[ɪnspekt]

verb

1. look over carefully. E.g.: **Please inspect your father's will carefully**
2. come to see in an official or professional capacity. [Syn: *visit*]

n (thing)	verb	adj	opposite
inspection	inspect	x	x
n (person)	**verb forms**	**adv**	**other**
inspector	inspected inspecting inspects	x	x

intense

[ɪntens]

adj

1. in an extreme degree. E.g.: **intense heat**, **intense anxiety**, **intense desire**, **intense emotion**, **the skunk's intense acrid odor**, **intense pain**, **enemy fire was intense**

n (thing)	verb	adj	opposite
intenseness intensification intension intensity	intensify	intense intensive	x
n (person)	**verb forms**	**adv**	**other**
x	intensified intensifies intensifying	intensely intensively	x

<u>Collocations from the ACL</u>
adj+n: high intensity, low intensity, intensive study.

---

manipulate

[mənɪpjəleɪt]

verb

1. hold something in one's hands and move it.
2. control (others or oneself) or influence skillfully, usually to one's advantage. E.g.: **She manipulates her boss** [Syn: *keep in line*, *control*]

n (thing)	verb	adj	opposite
manipulation	manipulate	manipulative	x
n (person)	**verb forms**	**adv**	**other**
x	manipulated manipulates manipulating	x	x

minimise

verb

1. make small or insignificant. [Syn: *minimize*]
2. represent as less significant or important. [Syn: *understate, minimize, downplay*]

n (thing)	**verb**	**adj**	**opposite**
x	minimise minimize	minimized	x
n (person)	**verb forms**	**adv**	**other**
x	minimised / -ized minimises / -izes minimising / -izing	x	x

---

nuclear

[nukliзr]

adj

1. of or relating to or constituting the nucleus of an atom. E.g.: **nuclear physics, nuclear fission, nuclear forces**
2. of or relating to or constituting the nucleus of a cell. E.g.: **nuclear membrane, nuclear division**
3. (weapons) deriving destructive energy from the release of atomic energy. E.g.: **nuclear war, nuclear weapons** [Syn: *atomic*]
4. constituting or like a nucleus. E.g.: **annexation of the suburban fringe by the nuclear metropolis, the nuclear core of the congregation**

n (thing)	**verb**	**adj**	**opposite**
x	x	nuclear	x
n (person)	**verb forms**	**adv**	**other**
x	x	x	x

<u>Collocations from the ACL</u>

adj+n: nuclear energy, nuclear family, nuclear power, nuclear war, nuclear weapon.

offset

[ɔfset]

verb

1. make up for. E.g.: **His skills offset his opponent's superior strength** [Syn: *cancel, set off*]
2. compensate for or counterbalance. E.g.: **offset deposits and withdrawals** [Syn: *countervail*]

noun

1. a compensating equivalent. [Syn: *counterbalance*]

n (thing)	**verb**	**adj**	**opposite**
offset	offset	x	x
n (person)	**verb forms**	**adv**	**other**
x	offset offsets offsetting	x	x

----

paragraph

[pærəgræf]

noun

1. one of several distinct subdivisions of a text intended to separate ideas; the beginning is usually marked by a new indented line.

n (thing)	**verb**	**adj**	**opposite**
paragraph paragraphing	x	x	x
n (person)	**verb forms**	**adv**	**other**
x	x	x	x

plus

[plʌs]

adj

1. on the positive side or higher end of a scale. E.g.: **a plus value, temperature of plus 5 degrees, a grade of C plus**
2. involving advantage or good. E.g.: **a plus (or positive) factor** [Syn: *positive*]

noun

1. a useful or valuable quality. [Syn: *asset*]
2. the arithmetic operation of summing; calculating the sum of two or more numbers. E.g.: **four plus three equals seven** [Syn: *summation, addition*]

n (thing)	**verb**	**adj**	**opposite**
plus	x	plus	x
n (person)	**verb forms**	**adv**	**other**
x	x	x	x

----

practitioner

[præktɪʃənɜr]

noun

1. someone who practices a learned profession. [Syn: *practician*]

n (thing)	**verb**	**adj**	**opposite**
x	x	x	x
n (person)	**verb forms**	**adv**	**other**
practitioner	x	x	x

predominant

[prɪdamənənt]

adj

1. having superior power and influence. E.g.: **the predominant mood among policy-makers is optimism** [Syn: *overriding, paramount, predominate, preponderant, preponderating*]
2. most frequent or common. [Syn: *prevailing*]

n (thing)	verb	adj	opposite
predominance	predominate	predominant predominate	x
n (person)	**verb forms**	**adv**	**other**
x	predominated predominates predominating	predominantly	x

----

prospect

[praspekt]

noun

1. the possibility of future success. E.g.: **his prospects as a writer are excellent**

n (thing)	verb	adj	opposite
prospect	x	prospective	x
n (person)	**verb forms**	**adv**	**other**
x	x	x	x

radical

[rædɪkəl]

adj

1. (used of opinions and actions) far beyond the norm. E.g.: **radical opinions on education** [Syn: *extremist, ultra*]
2. markedly new or introducing radical change. E.g.: **radical political views** [Syn: *revolutionary*]
3. arising from or going to the root. E.g.: **a radical flaw in the plan**

noun

1. an atom or group of atoms with at least one unpaired electron; in the body it is usually an oxygen molecule than has lost an electron and will stabilize itself by stealing an electron from a nearby molecule. E.g.: **in the body free radicals are high-energy part** [Syn: *free radical*]
2. a person who has radical ideas or opinions.

n (thing)	**verb**	**adj**	**opposite**
radical	x	radical	x
n (person)	**verb forms**	**adv**	**other**
radical	x	radically	x

<u>Collocations from the ACL</u>
adj+n: radical change, radical critique, radical differences, radical transformation.

random

[rændəm]

adj

1. lacking any definite plan or order or purpose; governed by or depending on chance. E.g.: **a random choice, bombs fell at random, random movements**

n (thing)	verb	adj	opposite
randomness	x	random	x
n (person)	**verb forms**	**adv**	**other**
x	x	randomly	x

Collocations from the ACL

adj+n: random error, random sample, random variable.

adv+vpp: (be) randomly assigned (to), (be) randomly chosen, (be) randomly selected.

---

reinforce

[riɪnfɔrs]

verb

1. strengthen and support with rewards. E.g.: **Let's reinforce good behavior** [Syn: *reward*]
2. make stronger. E.g.: **he reinforced the concrete** [Syn: *reenforce*]

n (thing)	verb	adj	opposite
reinforcement	reinforce	reinforced	x
n (person)	**verb forms**	**adv**	**other**
x	reinforced reinforces reinforcing	x	x

restore

[rɪstɔr]

verb

1. bring back into original existence, use, function, or position. E.g.: **restore law and order**, **restore the emperor to the throne** [Syn: *reinstate, reestablish*]
2. restore by replacing a part or putting together what is torn or broken. [Syn: *repair, mend, fix, bushel, doctor, furbish up, touch on*]

n (thing)	**verb**	**adj**	**opposite**
restoration	restore	x	x
n (person)	**verb forms**	**adv**	**other**
x	restored restores restoring	x	x

---

revise

[rɪvaɪz]

verb

1. make revisions in. E.g.: **revise a thesis**

n (thing)	**verb**	**adj**	**opposite**
revision	revise	x	x
n (person)	**verb forms**	**adv**	**other**
x	revised revises revising	x	x

Collocations from the ACL

adj+n: revised edition, revised version.

schedule

[skedʒʊl]

verb

1. make a schedule; plan the time and place for events. E.g.: **I scheduled an exam for this afternoon**

noun

1. an ordered list of times at which things are planned to occur.

n (thing)	verb	adj	opposite
schedule	schedule	x	unscheduled
n (person)	**verb forms**	**adv**	**other**
x	scheduled schedules scheduling	x	reschedule

----

tense

[tens]

adj

1. taut or rigid; stretched tight. E.g.: **tense piano strings**
2. in or of a state of physical or nervous tension.

noun

1. a grammatical category of verbs used to express distinctions of time.

n (thing)	verb	adj	opposite
tense tension	x	tense	x
n (person)	**verb forms**	**adv**	**other**
x	x	tensely	tenser tensest

terminate

[tɜrməneɪt]

verb

1. have an end, in a temporal, spatial, or quantitative sense; either spatial or metaphorical. E.g.: **the bronchioles terminate in a capillary bed** [Syn: *end, stop, finish, cease*]
2. bring to an end or halt. E.g.: **The attack on Poland terminated the relatively peaceful period after WWI** [Syn: *end*]

n (thing)	verb	adj	opposite
termination	terminate	terminal	x
n (person)	**verb forms**	**adv**	**other**
x	terminated terminates terminating	x	x

---

theme

[θim]

noun

1. the subject matter of a conversation or discussion. E.g.: **his letters were always on the theme of love** [Syn: *subject, topic*]
2. a unifying idea that is a recurrent element in a literary or artistic work. E.g.: **it was the usual `boy gets girl' theme** [Syn: *motif*]

n (thing)	verb	adj	opposite
theme	x	thematic	x
n (person)	**verb forms**	**adv**	**other**
x	x	thematically	x

<u>Collocations from the ACL</u>

adj+n: thematic analysis, central theme, common theme, key theme, main theme, major theme, recurrent theme.

thereby

[ðerbaɪ]

adv

1. by that means or because of that. E.g.: **He knocked over the red wine, thereby ruining the table cloth**

n (thing)	verb	adj	opposite
x	x	x	x
n (person)	**verb forms**	**adv**	**other**
x	x	thereby	x

----

uniform

[junəfɔrm]

adj

1. the same throughout in structure or composition. [Syn: *consistent*]

n (thing)	verb	adj	opposite
uniformity	x	uniform	x
n (person)	**verb forms**	**adv**	**other**
x	x	uniformly	x

vehicle

[vihɪkəl]

noun

1. a medium for the expression or achievement of something. E.g.: **his editorials provided a vehicle for his political views**
2. a conveyance that transports people or objects.

n (thing)	verb	adj	opposite
vehicle	x	x	x
n (person)	**verb forms**	**adv**	**other**
x	x	x	x

----

via

[vaɪə]

adj

1. going through a particular place (on the way to a destination).
2. using a particular means or person.

n (thing)	verb	adj	opposite
x	x	via	x
n (person)	**verb forms**	**adv**	**other**
x	x	x	x

----

virtual

[vɜrtʃuəl]

adj

1. being actually such in almost every respect. E.g.: **the once elegant temple lay in virtual ruin** [Syn: *practical*]

n (thing)	verb	adj	opposite
x	x	virtual	x
n (person)	**verb forms**	**adv**	**other**
x	x	virtually	x

visual

[vɪʒəwəl]

adj

1. able to be seen. E.g.: **a visual presentation**, **a visual image** [Syn: *ocular*]
2. relating to or using sight. E.g.: **visual powers**, **visual navigation** [Syn: *ocular, optic, optical*]

n (thing)	**verb**	**adj**	**opposite**
visualisation visualization	visualise visualize	visual	x
n (person)	**verb forms**	**adv**	**other**
x	visualised visualising visualized visualizing	visually	x

Collocations from the ACL

adj+n: visual image, visual media, visual perception, visual representation.

----

widespread

[waɪdspred]

adj

1. widely circulated or diffused. E.g.: **a widespread doctrine**, **widespread fear of nuclear war**

n (thing)	**verb**	**adj**	**opposite**
x	x	widespread	x
n (person)	**verb forms**	**adv**	**other**
x	x	x	x

Collocations from the ACL

adj+n: widespread acceptance, widespread belief, widespread support, widespread use.

Exercises (Sublist 8)

Task 1: Focus on Meaning #1

Study the following text on **Economic Growth**. Fill in the gaps using words from the box. All are words from AWL sublist 8. [Note: words from sublist 7 (underlined), sublist 9 (**bold**) and sublist 10 (***italics+bold***) are also shown, for review/preview purposes.]

accompany	crucial	denote	exploit
highlight	infrastructure	intense	minimise
predominant	prospect	thereby	via

Markets that allow personal and business rewards and incentives for increasing human and physical capital encourage overall macroeconomic growth. For example, workers have an incentive to acquire additional human capital, because additional education and skills give them the _____________ of higher wages. Firms have an incentive to invest in physical capital and in training workers, because this is usually _____________ by higher profits in the long run. Both individuals and firms seek to _____________ new technologies, because even small inventions can make work easier or lead to product improvement. Much of the rapid growth since the late nineteenth century has come from harnessing the power of competitive markets to allocate resources. This market orientation typically reaches beyond national borders and includes openness to international trade.

Despite a general market orientation, there remain _____________ roles for government to play. One of these is to correct failures in how capital and technology are allocated. In addition, government can guide or influence markets toward certain outcomes. The following examples _____________ some important areas that governments around the world have chosen to invest in to facilitate economic growth.

- The Danish government requires all children under 16 to attend school. They can choose to attend a public school (Folkeskole) or a private school. Students do not pay tuition to attend Folkeskole. Although primary/secondary (elementary/high) schools are _____________ public schools (87%), the private sector is growing, and one way the government encourages this is to supply vouchers to citizens who choose private school.
- In the United States, as in other countries, private investment is taxed. Low taxes encourage investment, and by choosing to _____________ tax revenue

in the private investment area, the government can encourage greater economic growth.

- The Japanese government in the mid-1990s undertook significant _____________ projects to improve roads and public works. This in turn increased the stock of physical capital and ultimately economic growth.
- The island of Mauritius is one of the few African nations to encourage international trade in government-supported Special Economic Zones. Special Economic Zones (SEZ) _____________ areas of the country, usually with access to a port where, among other benefits, the government does not tax sales, _____________ encouraging trade and allowing businesses to be more profitable. As a result of its SEZ status, Mauritius has enjoyed above-average economic growth since the 1980s.
- The European Union has strong programs to invest in scientific research. Firms which received support from their government increased their research _____________ and had more sales. Governments can support scientific research and technical training that helps to create and spread new technologies. They can also help inventors profit from their inventions _____________ legal measures such as protection of intellectual property rights.

Text adapted from Principles of Economics, Chapter 20 | Economic Growth © 2017 Rice University. Download for free at https://openstax.org/details/books/principles-economics.

Task 2: Focus on Meaning #2

Read the second part of the text on **Globalization**. Fill in the gaps using words from the box. All are words from AWL sublist 8. [Note: Words from sublist 7 (underlined), sublist 9 (**bold**) and sublist 10 (***italics+bold***) are again shown.]

accumulate	appreciate	commodity	contemporary
currency	inevitable	manipulate	offset
plus	widespread		

The continued protests during meetings of the World Trade Organization, the World Bank and the International Monetary Fund show that many people in _____________ society still fear world trade and globalization. While there are some definite disadvantages to globalization, most economists would agree that these are more than _____________ by the positives of the trend towards global trade.

The negatives of global trade include jobs lost due to imports or production shifting abroad, the fear of jobs being lost in this way, and the threat of companies exporting jobs if workers do not accept pay cuts. Sending domestic jobs to another country is called outsourcing. Many U.S. companies, such as Dell, IBM, and AT&T, have set up call service centers in India, the Philippines, and other countries. The practice of outsourcing is increasingly _____________, with even engineering and research and development jobs being outsourced. Outsourcing and "American jobs" were a big part of the 2016 presidential election, won by Donald Trump.

A closer look reveals that globalization has been the engine that creates jobs and wealth. The following are some of the main _____________ of global trade.

- Productivity grows more quickly when countries produce goods and services in which they have a comparative advantage, allowing living standards to increase.
- Global competition and importing cheap _____________ keep prices down, so inflation is less likely to stop economic growth. However, in some cases this is not working because countries _____________ the value of their _____________ to get a price advantage.
- An open economy spurs innovation with fresh ideas from abroad.
- Through infusion of foreign capital and technology, global trade provides poor countries with the chance to develop economically by spreading prosperity, although this does not always happen evenly, with more prosperous members of society tending to _____________ wealth more rapidly than the less prosperous.
- More information is shared between two trading partners that may not have much in common initially, including **insight** into local cultures and customs, which may help the two nations expand their collective knowledge and learn ways to compete globally.

In short, while there will _____________ be some disagreement over whether globalization is a positive trend, most economists _____________ that, on balance, the advantages outweigh the drawbacks.

Adapted from Introduction to Business, Chapter 3 Competing in the Global Marketplace © 2017 Rice University. Download for free at https://openstax.org/details/books/Introduction-Business.

Task 3: Focus on Meaning #3

The following sentences each contain an underlined word, which can be replaced by a synonym from the box below (synonyms in the box are all sublist 8 words). Replace each word with the correct synonym. An example has been done.

abandoned	appendices	charts	~~currency~~
guidelines	implicit	inevitably	paragraphs
practitioner	termination	vehicle	virtually

Example: The exchange rate is the price of one country's ***money*** *in terms of another country's.* __*currency*__

a) In economic theory, supply is limited, since resources are limited, whereas demand is **almost** unlimited. ________________

b) A copy of the consent form used in the survey is given in the **additional sections** at the end of the report. ________________

c) A plot of the results is shown in the two **diagrams** on the following page. ________________

d) Although the report did not directly accuse the manager of wrongdoing, there was **indirect** criticism of the way he acted. ________________

e) Before becoming chair of the genetics department, he was a medical **expert** in the specialising in viruses. ________________

f) The average U.S. household spends roughly one-third of its income on food and **car** expenses. ________________

g) Advances in technology will **in the end** lead to the loss of more manual jobs. ________________

h) The earlier hypothesis was **discarded** when two experiments failed to find supporting data. ________________

i) When conducting experiments involving people, ethical **recommendations** need to be followed very closely. ________________

j) Failure to deliver the good on time led to the **ending** of the contract. ________________

k) An academic essay requires you to organise your writing into separate **passages**, each of which should contain a clear topic and supporting ideas. ________________

Task 4: Collocations #1

Match the following words to form common collocations of AWL sublist 8 words. An example has been done for you.

nuclear	exploitation
change	study
revised	currency
dramatic	dramatically
intensive	energy
single	edition
economic	increase

Task 5: Collocations #2

The following are collocations for AWL sublist 8 words, taken from the ACL. Only *one* collocation matches the meaning of the sentence. Identify the correct collocation and cross out the incorrect one.

Example: He was randomly assigned/~~chosen~~/~~selected~~ to the group, though fortunately he found it easy to work with his fellow group members.

a) Although considered unsafe by some, **nuclear family/power/war/weapon** is a safe and reliable way to generate electricity for homes.
b) The idea that the colonization of Africa was a necessary evil is a **central/key/major/recurrent theme** in his writing. It appears in almost all of his books.
c) Despite their **radical changes/critiques/differences/transformations** on many issues, the two scholars managed to agree on an overall approach.
d) Safety with chemicals and apparatus is a **crucial difference/factor/importance/question** if any scientific experiment.
e) Gun control is a **contemporary debate/issue/life/society** that divides many people in the United States.
f) Fluctuations in the temperature during the experiment led to a significant **random error/sample/variable** in the measurements.

g) There is **widespread <u>acceptance/belief/support/use</u>** for stronger environmental powers by local governments.
h) Television is the most common form of **visual <u>image/media/perception/representation</u>** in our everyday lives.

Task 6: Word form #1

Complete the following sentences by changing the word form of the word(s) in brackets. An example has been done for you.

Example: Colonialism often resulted in the <u>exploitation</u> (exploit) of natural resources.

a) Employees will be ______________ (automate) enrolled in the scheme unless they voluntarily opt out.
b) He was chosen to resolve the dispute since he was completely ______________ (bias). He did not have any reason to favour either side.
c) The two methods were ______________ (complement) and combined together to enable greater accuracy in measuring results.
d) Since the two sets of results were ______________ (contradict), a third experiment was conducted to see which set were valid.
e) The metal ______________ (detect) aided in the discovery of Saxon treasure at the site.
f) Managers need to monitor the implementation of a plan and make corrections to any ______________ (deviate) in the plan.
g) Children in the group under study were rewarded when they ______________ (exhibit) positive behaviour.
h) Errors in measurement were likely the result of ______________ (fluctuate) in the temperature.
i) All of the new staff members were required to attend the ______________ (induce) events in the first week.
j) The safety ______________ (inspect) decided that the building was unfit for use. They ordered it to be closed down.
k) The ______________ (restore) of the public hall damaged by fire was proceeding as planned.
l) Since fewer than half of the members were present for the meeting, they decided to ______________ (schedule).

Task 7: Word form #2

Change the following words to make the *noun* form, and add them to the appropriate place on the diagram according to the noun suffix which is used. An example has been done for you (eventual->*eventuality*). *Be careful of spelling when making the noun forms.*

ambiguous	arbitrary	clarify	conform
displace	drama	eventual	~~intense~~
random	reinforce	revise	tense
uniform	visual		

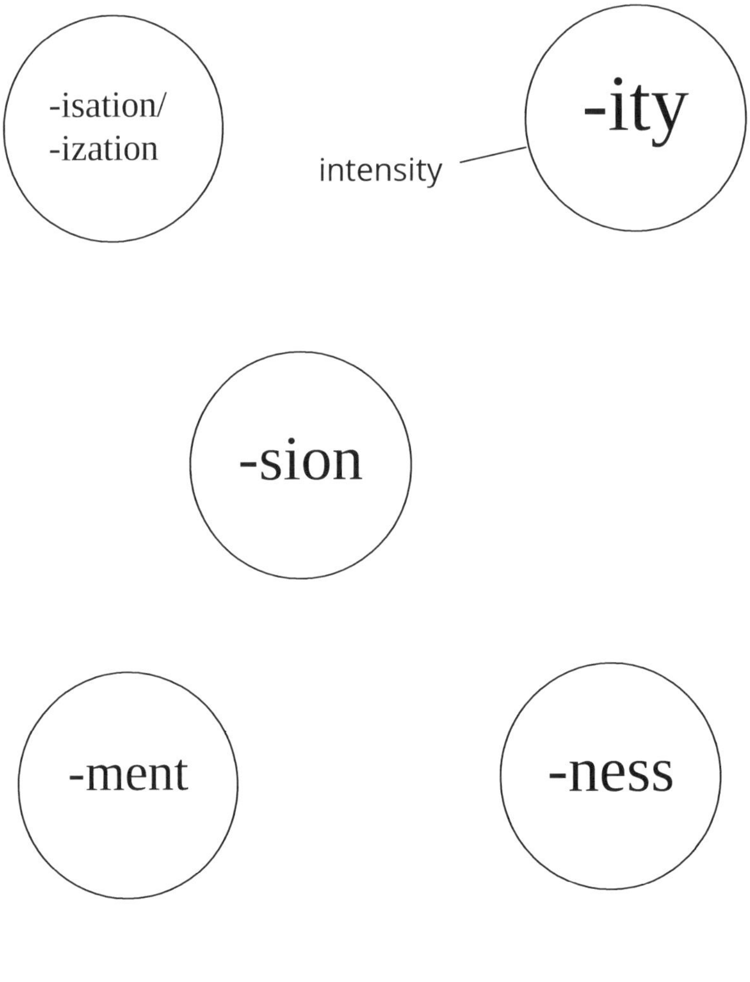

Academic Word List:

Sublist 9

accommodate

[əkɑmədeɪt]

verb

1. provide housing for. [Syn: *lodge*]
2. be agreeable or acceptable to. [Syn: *suit*, *fit*]
3. make compatible with. E.g.: **The scientists had to accommodate the new results with the existing theories** [Syn: *reconcile*, *conciliate*]

n (thing)	verb	adj	opposite
accommodation	accommodate	accommodating	x
n (person)	**verb forms**	**adv**	**other**
x	accommodated accommodates accommodating	x	x

---

analogy

[ənælədʒi]

noun

1. drawing a comparison in order to show a similarity in some respect. E.g.: **the operation of a computer presents and interesting analogy to the working of the brain, the models show by analogy how matter is built up**

n (thing)	verb	adj	opposite
analogy	x	analogous	x
n (person)	**verb forms**	**adv**	**other**
x	x	x	x

anticipate

[æntɪsəpeɪt]

verb

1. act in advance of; deal with ahead of time. [Syn: *foresee, forestall, counter*]
2. make a prediction about; tell in advance. [Syn: *predict, foretell, prognosticate, call, forebode, promise*]

n (thing)	**verb**	**adj**	**opposite**
anticipation	anticipate	x	unanticipated
n (person)	**verb forms**	**adv**	**other**
x	anticipated anticipates anticipating	x	x

----

assure

[əʃʊr]

verb

1. make certain of. [Syn: *guarantee, ensure, insure, secure*]

n (thing)	**verb**	**adj**	**opposite**
assurance	assure	x	x
n (person)	**verb forms**	**adv**	**other**
x	assured assures assuring	assuredly	x

attain

[əteɪn]

verb

1. to gain with effort. [Syn: *achieve, accomplish, reach*]
2. reach a destination, either real or abstract. [Syn: *reach, make, hit, arrive at, gain*]

n (thing)	**verb**	**adj**	**opposite**
attainment	attain	attainable	unattainable
n (person)	**verb forms**	**adv**	**other**
x	attained attaining attains	x	x

----

behalf

[bɪhæf]

noun

1. as the agent of or on someone's part (usually expressed as "on behalf of" rather than "in behalf of"). E.g.: **the guardian signed the contract on behalf of the minor child, this letter is written on behalf of my client;**

n (thing)	**verb**	**adj**	**opposite**
behalf	x	x	x
n (person)	**verb forms**	**adv**	**other**
x	x	x	x

bulk

[bʌlk]

noun

1. the property of something that is great in magnitude. E.g.: **it is cheaper to buy it in bulk** [Syn: *mass, volume*]
2. the property resulting from being or relating to the greater in number of two parts; the main part. E.g.: **the bulk of the work is finished** [Syn: *majority*]
3. the property possessed by a large mass.

n (thing)	**verb**	**adj**	**opposite**
bulk	x	bulky	x
n (person)	**verb forms**	**adv**	**other**
x	x	x	x

---

cease

[sis]

verb

1. have an end, in a temporal, spatial, or quantitative sense; either spatial or metaphorical. [Syn: *end, stop, finish, terminate*]
2. put an end to a state or an activity. [Syn: *discontinue, stop, give up, quit, lay off*]

n (thing)	**verb**	**adj**	**opposite**
x	cease	x	ceaseless
n (person)	**verb forms**	**adv**	**other**
x	ceased ceases ceasing	x	x

coherent

[koʊhɪrənt]

adj

1. capable of thinking and expressing yourself in a clear and consistent manner. E.g.: **she was more coherent than she had been just after the accident** [Syn: *logical, lucid*]
2. marked by an orderly, logical, and aesthetically consistent relation of parts. E.g.: **a coherent argument**
3. sticking together. E.g.: **two coherent sheets** [Syn: *tenacious*]

n (thing)	verb	adj	opposite
coherence	x	coherent	incoherent incoherently
n (person)	**verb forms**	**adv**	**other**
x	x	coherently	x

---

coincide

[koʊɪnsaɪd]

verb

1. be the same. E.g.: **our views on this matter coincided**
2. happen simultaneously. E.g.: **The two events coincided** [Syn: *concur*]

n (thing)	verb	adj	opposite
coincidence	coincide	coincident coincidental coinciding	x
n (person)	**verb forms**	**adv**	**other**
x	coincided coincides coinciding	x	x

commence

[kəmens]

verb

1. set in motion, cause to start. [Syn: *begin*, *lead off*, *start*]

n (thing)	**verb**	**adj**	**opposite**
commencement	commence	x	x
n (person)	**verb forms**	**adv**	**other**
x	commenced commences commencing	x	x

---

compatible

[kəmpætəbəl]

adj

1. able to exist and perform in harmonious or agreeable combination. E.g.: **a compatible married couple, her deeds were compatible with her ideology**
2. capable of being used with or connected to other devices or components without modification.

n (thing)	**verb**	**adj**	**opposite**
compatibility	x	compatible	incompatibility incompatible
n (person)	**verb forms**	**adv**	**other**
x	x	x	x

concurrent

[kənkɜrənt]

adj

1. occurring or operating at the same time. [Syn: *coincident, coincidental, coinciding, cooccurring, simultaneous*]

n (thing)	verb	adj	opposite
x	x	concurrent	x
n (person)	**verb forms**	**adv**	**other**
x	x	concurrently	x

---

confine

[kənfaɪn]

verb

1. deprive of freedom; take into confinement. [Syn: *detain*]
2. to close within bounds, limit or hold back from movement. [Syn: *restrain, hold*]
3. place limits on (extent or access). [Syn: *restrict, restrain, trammel, limit, bound, throttle*]

n (thing)	verb	adj	opposite
x	confine	x	unconfined
n (person)	**verb forms**	**adv**	**other**
x	confined confines confining	x	x

controversy

[kantrəv3rsi]

noun

1. a contentious speech act; a dispute where there is strong disagreement. [Syn: *contention*, *contestation*, *disputation*, *disceptation*, *tilt*, *argument*, *arguing*]

n (thing)	verb	adj	opposite
controversy	x	controversial	uncontroversial
n (person)	**verb forms**	**adv**	**other**
x	x	controversially	x

----

converse

[kanv3rs]

adj

1. of words so related that one reverses the relation denoted by the other. E.g.: **`parental' and `filial' are converse terms**

noun

1. a proposition obtained by conversion.

n (thing)	verb	adj	opposite
converse	x	converse	x
n (person)	**verb forms**	**adv**	**other**
x	x	conversely	x

device

[dɪvaɪs]

noun

1. an instrumentality invented for a particular purpose. E.g.: **the device is small enough to wear on your wrist, a device intended to conserve water**

n (thing)	verb	adj	opposite
device	x	x	x
n (person)	**verb forms**	**adv**	**other**
x	x	x	x

---

devote

[dɪvoʊt]

verb

1. give entirely to a specific person, activity, or cause. [Syn: *give, dedicate, consecrate, commit*]

n (thing)	verb	adj	opposite
devotion	devote	devoted	x
n (person)	**verb forms**	**adv**	**other**
x	devoted devotes devoting	devotedly	x

diminish

[dɪmɪnɪʃ]

verb

1. decrease in size, extent, or range. [Syn: *decrease, lessen, fall*]

n (thing)	verb	adj	opposite
diminution	diminish	x	undiminished
n (person)	**verb forms**	**adv**	**other**
x	diminished diminishes diminishing	x	x

---

distort

[dɪstɔrt]

verb

1. alter the shape of (something) by stress. [Syn: *deform, strain*]
2. make false by mutilation or addition; as of a message or story. [Syn: *falsify, garble, warp*]

n (thing)	verb	adj	opposite
distortion	distort	distorted	x
n (person)	**verb forms**	**adv**	**other**
x	distorted distorting distorts	x	x

duration

[dʊreɪʃən]

noun

1. the period of time during which something continues. [Syn: *continuance*]
2. continuance in time. E.g.: **the ceremony was of short duration** [Syn: *length*]

n (thing)	verb	adj	opposite
duration	x	x	x
n (person)	**verb forms**	**adv**	**other**
x	x	x	x

Collocations from the ACL
adj+n: long duration, maximum duration, short duration.

---

erode

[ɪroʊd]

verb

1. remove soil or rock. E.g.: **Rain eroded the terraces** [Syn: *eat away*, *fret*]
2. become ground down or deteriorate. E.g.: **Her confidence eroded** [Syn: *gnaw*, *gnaw at*, *eat at*, *wear away*]

n (thing)	verb	adj	opposite
erosion	erode	eroded	x
n (person)	**verb forms**	**adv**	**other**
x	eroded erodes eroding	x	x

ethic

[eθɪk]

noun

1. the principles of right and wrong that are accepted by an individual or a social group. E.g.: **the Puritan ethic** [Syn: *moral principle, value-system, value orientation*]
2. a system of principles governing morality and acceptable conduct. [Syn: *ethical code*]

n (thing)	verb	adj	opposite
ethic ethics	x	ethical	unethical
n (person)	**verb forms**	**adv**	**other**
x	x	ethically	x

<u>Collocations from the ACL</u>

adj+n: ethical consideration, ethical dilemma, ethical issue, ethical principle, ethical problem, ethical question.

---

format

[fɔrmæt]

verb

1. set (printed matter) into a specific format. [Syn: *arrange*]

noun

1. the general appearance of a publication.

n (thing)	verb	adj	opposite
format	format	x	x
n (person)	**verb forms**	**adv**	**other**
x	formats formatted formatting	x	x

<u>Collocations from the ACL</u>

v+n: follow (a) format, use (a) format.

found

[faʊnd]

verb

1. set up or lay the groundwork for. [Syn: *establish, plant, constitute, institute*]

n (thing)	verb	adj	opposite
x	found	x	unfounded
n (person)	**verb forms**	**adv**	**other**
founder	founded founding	x	x

Collocations from the ACL

adv+vpp: (be) commonly found (in), (be) frequently found, (be) generally found.

----

inherent

[ɪnherənt]

adj

1. present at birth but not necessarily hereditary; acquired during fetal development. [Syn: *congenital, inborn, innate*]
2. existing as an essential constituent or characteristic. [Syn: *built-in, constitutional, inbuilt, integral*]
3. in the nature of something though not readily apparent. E.g.: **shortcomings inherent in our approach** [Syn: *implicit in, underlying*]

n (thing)	verb	adj	opposite
x	x	inherent	x
n (person)	**verb forms**	**adv**	**other**
x	x	inherently	x

insight

[ɪnsaɪt]

noun

1. a feeling of understanding. [Syn: *perceptiveness, perceptivity*]
2. the clear (and often sudden) understanding of a complex situation. [Syn: *brainstorm, brainwave*]

n (thing)	**verb**	**adj**	**opposite**
insight	x	insightful	x
n (person)	**verb forms**	**adv**	**other**
x	x	x	x

Collocations from the ACL
v+n: gain insight (into), give insight (into), offer insight (into), provide insight (into).

---

integral

[ɪntəgrəl]

adj

1. existing as an essential constituent or characteristic. [Syn: *built-in, constitutional, inbuilt, inherent*]

n (thing)	**verb**	**adj**	**opposite**
x	x	integral	x
n (person)	**verb forms**	**adv**	**other**
x	x	x	x

intermediate

[ɪntɜrmidiɪt]

adj

1. around the middle of a scale of evaluation of physical measures. E.g.: **intermediate capacity, a plane with intermediate range** [Syn: *average*, *medium*]
2. lying between two extremes in time or space or degree. E.g.: **going from sitting to standing without intermediate pushes with the hands, intermediate stages in a process, intermediate stops on the route, an intermediate level**

n (thing)	verb	adj	opposite
x	x	intermediate	x
n (person)	**verb forms**	**adv**	**other**
x	x	x	x

----

manual

[mænjuəl]

adj

1. of or relating to the hands. E.g.: **manual dexterity**
2. doing or requiring physical work. E.g.: **manual labor, manual laborer**

noun

1. a small handbook.

n (thing)	verb	adj	opposite
manual	x	manual	x
n (person)	**verb forms**	**adv**	**other**
x	x	manually	x

mature

[mətʃʊr]

adj

1. having reached full natural growth or development. E.g.: **a mature cell**
2. fully developed or matured and ready to be eaten or used. E.g.: **full-bodies mature wines** [Syn: *ripe*]
3. fully considered and perfected. E.g.: **mature plans** [Syn: *matured*]

verb

1. cause to ripen or develop fully. E.g.: **Age matures a good wine** [Syn: *ripen*]
2. develop and reach maturity; undergo maturation. E.g.: **He matured fast** [Syn: *maturate, grow*]

n (thing)	**verb**	**adj**	**opposite**
maturation maturity	mature	maturational mature	immature immaturity
n (person)	**verb forms**	**adv**	**other**
x	matured matures maturing	x	x

---

mediate

[midieɪt]

verb

1. act between parties with a view to reconciling differences. E.g.: **He mediated a settlement** [Syn: *intercede, intermediate, liaise, arbitrate*]

n (thing)	**verb**	**adj**	**opposite**
mediation	mediate	x	x
n (person)	**verb forms**	**adv**	**other**
x	mediated mediates mediating	x	x

medium

[midiəm]

adj

1. around the middle of a scale of evaluation of physical measures. E.g.: **medium bombers** [Syn: *average, intermediate*]

noun

1. a state that is intermediate between extremes; a middle position. E.g.: **a happy medium**
2. an intervening substance through which signals can travel as a means for communication.
3. transmissions that are disseminated widely to the public. [Syn: *mass medium*]

n (thing)	**verb**	**adj**	**opposite**
medium	x	medium	x
n (person)	**verb forms**	**adv**	**other**
x	x	x	x

----

military

[mɪləteri]

adj

1. associated with or performed by armed services as contrasted with civilians. E.g.: **military police**
2. characteristic of or associated with soldiers or the military. E.g.: **military uniforms**

n (thing)	**verb**	**adj**	**opposite**
x	x	military	x
n (person)	**verb forms**	**adv**	**other**
x	x	x	x

<u>Collocations from the ACL</u>

adj+n: military action, military force, military power, military service.

minimal

[mɪnəməl]

adj

1. the least possible. E.g.: **needed to enforce minimal standards, her grades were minimal, a minimal charge for the service** [Syn: *minimum*]

n (thing)	verb	adj	opposite
minimalisation minimalization	minimalise minimalize	minimal minimalist minimalistic	x
n (person)	**verb forms**	**adv**	**other**
minimalist	minimalised / -ized minimalises / -izes minimalising / -izing	minimally	x

---

mutual

[mjutʃuəl]

adj

1. concerning each of two or more persons or things; especially given or done in return. E.g.: **mutual respect** [Syn: *reciprocal*]
2. common to or shared by two or more parties. E.g.: **the mutual interests of management and labor** [Syn: *common*]

n (thing)	verb	adj	opposite
x	x	mutual	x
n (person)	**verb forms**	**adv**	**other**
x	x	mutually	x

Collocations from the ACL

adj+n: mutual recognition, mutual support, mutual trust, mutual understanding.

norm

[nɔrm]

noun

1. a standard or model or pattern regarded as typical. E.g.: **the current middle-class norm of two children per family**

n (thing)	verb	adj	opposite
norm	x	x	x
n (person)	**verb forms**	**adv**	**other**
x	x	x	x

Collocations from the ACL
adj+n: cultural norm, social norm.

---

overlap

[oʊvɜrlæp]

verb

1. coincide partially or wholly. E.g.: **Our vacations overlap**
2. extend over and cover a part of. E.g.: **The roofs of the houses overlap in this crowded city**

noun

1. a representation of common ground between theories or phenomena. E.g.: **there was no overlap between their proposals** [Syn: *convergence, intersection*]

n (thing)	verb	adj	opposite
overlap	overlap	x	x
n (person)	**verb forms**	**adv**	**other**
x	overlapped overlapping overlaps	x	x

passive

[pæsɪv]

adj

1. peacefully resistant in response to injustice. E.g.: **passive resistance** [Syn: *peaceful*]
2. lacking in energy or will. E.g.: **Much benevolence of the passive order may be traced to a disinclination to inflict pain upon oneself- George Meredith** [Syn: *inactive*]

n (thing)	verb	adj	opposite
passivity	x	passive	x
n (person)	**verb forms**	**adv**	**other**
x	x	passively	x

---

portion

[pɔrʃən]

noun

1. something determined in relation to something that includes it. E.g.: **I read a portion of the manuscript** [Syn: *part, component part, component*]
2. the result of parcelling out or sharing. [Syn: *parcel, share*]

n (thing)	verb	adj	opposite
portion	x	x	x
n (person)	**verb forms**	**adv**	**other**
x	x	x	x

Collocations from the ACL

adj+n: large portion, significant portion, small portion.

preliminary

[prɪlɪməneri]

adj

1. designed to orient or acquaint with a situation before proceeding. E.g.: **a preliminary investigation**

noun

1. something that serves as a preceding event or introduces what follows. E.g.: **training is a necessary preliminary to employment** [Syn: *overture*, *prelude*]

n (thing)	verb	adj	opposite
preliminary	x	preliminary	x
n (person)	**verb forms**	**adv**	**other**
x	x	x	x

Collocations from the ACL
adj+n: preliminary data, preliminary findings, preliminary result.

---

protocol

[proʊtəkɑl]

noun

1. code of correct conduct. E.g.: **safety protocols, academic protocol**

n (thing)	verb	adj	opposite
protocol	x	x	x
n (person)	**verb forms**	**adv**	**other**
x	x	x	x

qualitative

[kwaləteɪtɪv]

adj

1. involving distinctions based on qualities. E.g.: **qualitative change**, **qualitative data**, **qualitative analysis determines the chemical constituents of a substance or mixture**

n (thing)	verb	adj	opposite
x	x	qualitative	x
n (person)	**verb forms**	**adv**	**other**
x	x	qualitatively	x

Collocations from the ACL

adj+n: qualitative analysis, qualitative approach, qualitative data, qualitative method, qualitative research, qualitative study.

---

refine

[rəfaɪn]

verb

1. make more complex, intricate, or richer. E.g.: **refine a design or pattern** [Syn: *complicate*, *rarify*, *elaborate*]
2. make more precise or increase the discriminatory powers of. E.g.: **refine a method of analysis**, **refine the constant in the equation**

n (thing)	verb	adj	opposite
refinement	refine	x	x
n (person)	**verb forms**	**adv**	**other**
x	refined refines refining	x	x

relax

[rɪlæks]

verb

1. become less severe or strict. E.g.: **The rules relaxed after the new director arrived** [Syn: *loosen*]
2. make less severe or strict. E.g.: **The government relaxed the curfew after most of the rebels were caught** [Syn: *loosen*]
3. become less tense, less formal, or less restrained, and assume a friendlier manner. E.g.: **our new colleague relaxed when he saw that we were a friendly group** [Syn: *loosen up*]
4. become loose or looser or less tight. E.g.: **the rope relaxed** [Syn: *loosen, loose*]

n (thing)	**verb**	**adj**	**opposite**
relaxation	relax	relaxed relaxing	x
n (person)	**verb forms**	**adv**	**other**
x	relaxed relaxes relaxing	x	x

----

restrain

[ristreɪn]

verb

1. keep under control; keep in check. [Syn: *suppress, keep, keep back, hold back*]
2. place limits on (extent or access). [Syn: *restrict, trammel, limit, bound, confine, throttle*]

n (thing)	**verb**	**adj**	**opposite**
restraint	restrain	x	unrestrained
n (person)	**verb forms**	**adv**	**other**
x	restrained restraining restrains	x	x

revolution

[revəluʃən]

noun

1. a drastic and far-reaching change in ways of thinking and behaving. E.g.: **the industrial revolution was also a cultural revolution**
2. a single complete turn (axial or orbital). E.g.: **the revolution of the earth about the sun takes one year** [Syn: *rotation*, *gyration*]
3. the overthrow of a government by those who are governed.

n (thing)	verb	adj	opposite
revolution	revolutionise revolutionize	revolutionary	x
n (person)	**verb forms**	**adv**	**other**
revolutionary revolutionist	revolutionised / -ized revolutionises / -izes revolutionising / -izing	x	x

---

rigid

[rɪdʒəd]

adj

1. incapable of compromise or flexibility. [Syn: *strict*]
2. incapable of or resistant to bending. E.g.: **a rigid strip of metal, a table made of rigid plastic** [Syn: *stiff*]
3. incapable of adapting or changing to meet circumstances. E.g.: **a rigid disciplinarian** [Syn: *inflexible*, *unbending*]

n (thing)	verb	adj	opposite
rigidity	x	rigid	x
n (person)	**verb forms**	**adv**	**other**
x	x	rigidly	x

route

[rut]

verb

1. send via a specific route.

noun

1. an established line of travel or access. [Syn: *path*, *itinerary*]

n (thing)	verb	adj	opposite
route	route	x	x
n (person)	**verb forms**	**adv**	**other**
x	routed routes routing	x	x

----

scenario

[sɪnerioʊ]

noun

1. a postulated sequence of possible events. E.g.: **planners developed several scenarios in case of an attack**

n (thing)	verb	adj	opposite
scenario	x	x	x
n (person)	**verb forms**	**adv**	**other**
x	x	x	x

sphere

[sfɪr]

noun

1. a three-dimensional closed surface such that every point on the surface is equidistant from the center.
2. a particular aspect of life or activity. [Syn: *sector*]
3. any spherically shaped artifact.

n (thing)	**verb**	**adj**	**opposite**
sphere	x	spherical	x
n (person)	**verb forms**	**adv**	**other**
x	x	spherically	x

Collocations from the ACL

adj+n: domestic sphere, private sphere, public sphere.

---

subordinate

[səbɔrdəneɪt]

adj

1. subject or submissive to authority or the control of another. E.g.: **a subordinate kingdom**
2. inferior in rank or status. E.g.: **a subordinate functionary** [Syn: *petty, junior-grade, inferior, lower, lower-ranking, lowly, secondary, subaltern*]

noun

1. an assistant subject to the authority or control of another. [Syn: *subsidiary, underling, foot soldier*]

n (thing)	**verb**	**adj**	**opposite**
subordinate subordination	x	subordinate	x
n (person)	**verb forms**	**adv**	**other**
x	x	x	x

supplement

[sʌpləmənt]

verb

1. serve as a supplement to. E.g.: **Vitamins supplemented his meager diet**

noun

1. a quantity added (e.g. to make up for a deficiency). [Syn: *supplementation*]

n (thing)	**verb**	**adj**	**opposite**
supplement	supplement	supplementary	x
n (person)	**verb forms**	**adv**	**other**
x	supplemented supplementing supplements	x	x

---

suspend

[səspend]

verb

1. bar temporarily; from school, office, etc. [Syn: *debar*]
2. hang freely. E.g.: **The secret police suspended their victims from the ceiling and beat them**
3. make inoperative or stop. E.g.: **suspend payments on the loan** [Syn: *set aside*]

n (thing)	**verb**	**adj**	**opposite**
suspension	suspend	suspended	x
n (person)	**verb forms**	**adv**	**other**
x	suspended suspending suspends	x	x

team

[tim]

verb

1. form a team. E.g.: **We teamed up for this new project** [Syn: *team up*]

noun

1. a cooperative unit. [Syn: *squad*]

n (thing)	verb	adj	opposite
team	team	x	x
n (person)	**verb forms**	**adv**	**other**
x	teamed teaming teams	x	x

----

temporary

[tempɜreri]

adj

1. not permanent; not lasting. E.g.: **temporary housing** [Syn: *impermanent*]

n (thing)	verb	adj	opposite
x	x	temporary	x
n (person)	**verb forms**	**adv**	**other**
x	x	temporarily	x

trigger

[trɪgɜr]

verb

1. put in motion or move to act. E.g.: **trigger a reaction** [Syn: *trip, actuate, activate, set off, spark off, spark, trigger off, touch off*]

noun

1. an act that sets in motion some course of events. [Syn: *induction, initiation*]

n (thing)	verb	adj	opposite
trigger	trigger	x	x
n (person)	**verb forms**	**adv**	**other**
x	triggered triggering triggers	x	x

----

unify

[junəfaɪ]

verb

1. become one. E.g.: **Will the two Koreas unify?** [Syn: *unite, merge*]
2. join or combine. [Syn: *unite, merge*]

n (thing)	verb	adj	opposite
unification	unify	unified unifying	x
n (person)	**verb forms**	**adv**	**other**
x	unified unifies unifying	x	x

violate

[vaɪəleɪt]

verb

1. act in disregard of laws and rules. E.g.: **violate the basic laws or human civilization** [Syn: *transgress, offend, infract, go against, breach, break*]

n (thing)	verb	adj	opposite
violation	violate	x	x
n (person)	**verb forms**	**adv**	**other**
x	violated violates violating	x	x

----

vision

[vɪʒən]

noun

1. the ability to see; the faculty of vision. [Syn: *sight, visual sense, visual modality*]
2. the perceptual experience of seeing. E.g.: **the runners emerged from the trees into his clear vision** [Syn: *visual sensation*]
3. a vivid mental image. E.g.: **he had a vision of his own death**

n (thing)	verb	adj	opposite
vision	x	x	x
n (person)	**verb forms**	**adv**	**other**
x	x	x	x

Exercises (Sublist 9)

Task 1: Focus on Meaning #1

Study the following text on **Medical Imaging**. Fill in the gaps using words from the box. All are words from AWL sublist 9. [Note: words from sublist 7 (<u>underlined</u>), sublist 8 (*italics*) and **sublist 10** (***italics+bold***) are also shown, for review/preview purposes.]

confined	device	duration	inherent
minimal	refinements	revolutionized	trigger

It was not until the late nineteenth century that medical researchers discovered non-surgical methods to look inside the living body. The first of these techniques was the X-ray, a form of high energy electromagnetic radiation with a short wavelength capable of penetrating solids and ionizing gases. X-rays are best used to *visualize* hard body structures such as teeth and bones. Like many forms of high energy radiation, however, X-rays are capable of damaging cells and initiating changes that can lead to cancer. This danger of excessive exposure to X-rays was not fully *appreciated* for many years after their *widespread* use. _____________ and enhancements of X-ray techniques have continued throughout the twentieth and twenty-first centuries, and effective shielding and limiting exposure mean the danger of irradiation to the patient and the operator is now _____________.

X-rays can depict a two-dimensional image of a body region, and only from a single angle. In contrast, more recent medical imaging technologies produce data that is integrated and analyzed by computers to produce three-dimensional images or images that reveal aspects of body functioning. The main ones are: computed tomography; magnetic resonance imaging; positron emission tomography; and ultrasonography.

Tomography refers to imaging by sections. Computed tomography (CT) is a noninvasive imaging technique that uses computers to analyze several cross-sectional X-rays in order to reveal minute details about structures in the body. Invented in the 1970s, CT scanning is routine for many types of diagnostic evaluations. Its level of detail is so precise that it can allow physicians to measure the size of a mass down to a millimeter. The main disadvantage of CT scanning is that it exposes patients to a dose of radiation many times higher than that of X-rays. In fact, children who ***undergo*** CT scans are at increased risk of developing cancer, as are <u>adults</u> who have multiple CT scans.

Magnetic resonance imaging (MRI) is a noninvasive medical imaging technique based on an ____________ property of matter, discovered by *nuclear* physicists in the 1930s, which is that when matter is exposed to magnetic fields and radio waves, it emits radio signals. In 1970, a physician and researcher named Raymond Damadian noticed that malignant (cancerous) tissue gave off different signals than normal body tissue. He applied for a patent for the first MRI scanning ____________, which was in use clinically by the early 1980s. MRI allows for precise imaging, and is especially useful in discovering tumours. MRI has the major advantage of not exposing patients to radiation. Drawbacks of MRI scans include their much higher cost, and patient discomfort with the procedure. The MRI scanner subjects the patient to such powerful electromagnets that the scan room must be shielded, and the patient must be enclosed in a metal tube-like scanner for the ____________ of the scan, sometimes as long as thirty minutes. Being ____________ in such a small space can be uncomfortable and impractical for ill patients. The scanner is also extremely noisy, which can ____________ anxiety or fear in patients. These problems have been overcome somewhat with the development of "open" MRI scanning, which does not require the patient to be entirely enclosed in the metal tube.

Positron emission tomography (PET) is a medical imaging technique involving the use of ***so-called*** radiopharmaceuticals, substances that emit radiation that is short-lived and therefore relatively safe to administer to the body. Although the first PET scanner was introduced in 1961, it took 15 more years before radiopharmaceuticals were combined with the technique and ____________ its potential. The main advantage is that PET can illustrate physiologic activity of the organ or organs being targeted, including nutrient metabolism and blood flow, whereas CT and MRI scans can only show static images. PET is widely used to diagnose a multitude of conditions, such as heart disease, the spread of cancer, certain forms of infection, brain abnormalities, bone disease, and thyroid disease.

Ultrasonography is an imaging technique that uses the transmission of high-frequency sound waves into the body to generate an echo signal that is converted by a computer into a real-time image of anatomy and physiology. Ultrasonography is the least invasive of all imaging techniques, and it is therefore used more freely in sensitive situations such as pregnancy. The main disadvantages of ultrasonography are that the image quality is heavily operator-dependent and that it is unable to penetrate bone and gas.

Task 2: Focus on Meaning #2

Read the following text, with information on **Research Ethics**. Fill in the gaps using words from the box. All are words from AWL sublist 9. [Note: words from sublist 7 (underlined), **sublist 8** (**bold**) and sublist 10 (***italics+bold***) are again shown, for review/preview purposes.]

assurances	behalf	commence	distort
ethical x3	ethically	integral	protocols
qualitative	suspend	violate	

Today, scientists agree that good research is _____________ in nature and is guided by a basic respect for human dignity and safety. However, this has not always been the case. Modern researchers must demonstrate that the research they perform is _____________ sound.

RESEARCH INVOLVING HUMAN PARTICIPANTS

Any experiment involving the participation of human subjects is governed by extensive, strict **guidelines** designed to ensure that the experiment does not result in harm. Any research institution that receives federal support for research involving human participants must have access to an institutional review board (IRB). The IRB is a committee of individuals often made up of members of the institution's administration, scientists, and community members. The purpose of the IRB is to review proposals for research that involves human participants, and approval from the IRB is required before any such experiment can _____________.

One _____________ component of any experiment approved by an institution's IRB is an informed consent form, which must be signed by each participant before they can take part in the experiment. An informed consent form provides a written description of what participants can expect during the experiment, including potential risks and implications of the research. It also gives _____________ about the voluntary nature of the research, and confidentiality of data collection. In cases where research participants are under the age of 18, the parents or legal guardians are required to sign the form on _____________ of their child.

Pioneer German sociologist Max Weber (1864–1920) identified another **crucial** _____________ concern. Social science research often uses _____________ data, for example from case studies or ethnographies, rather than statistical data. Weber stated that researchers must remain impartial or 'value neutral', without **bias** or judgment, during the course of a study and when interpreting and publishing results. They are obligated to disclose research findings and should not omit or _____________ significant data. Many researchers believe, however, that it is impossible to set aside personal values and retain complete objectivity. They caution readers, rather, to understand that social science studies may, by necessity, contain a certain amount of value **bias**. It does not discredit the results but allows readers to view them as one form of truth rather than a singular fact.

RESEARCH INVOLVING ANIMAL SUBJECTS

Many psychologists conduct research involving animal subjects. Often, these researchers use rodents or birds as the subjects of their experiments; the APA estimates that 90% of all animal research in psychology uses these species (American Psychological Association, n.d.). Because many basic processes in animals are sufficiently similar to those in humans, these animals are acceptable substitutes for research that would be considered ____________ in human participants.

This does not mean that animal researchers are immune to ____________ concerns. Indeed, the humane treatment of animal research subjects is a critical aspect of this type of research. Researchers must design their experiments to **minimize** any pain or distress experienced by animals serving as research subjects.

Whereas IRBs review research proposals that involve human participants, animal experimental proposals are reviewed by an Institutional Animal Care and Use Committee (IACUC). An IACUC consists of institutional administrators, scientists, veterinarians, and community members. This committee is charged with ensuring that all experimental proposals require the humane treatment of animal research subjects. It also conducts semi-annual **inspections** of all animal facilities to ensure that the research ____________ are being followed, and has the power to ____________ or halt any experiments which ____________ its regulations. No animal research project can proceed without the committee's approval.

Task 3: Focus on Meaning #3

The following sentences each contain an underlined word, which can be replaced by a synonym from the box below (synonyms in the box are all sublist 9 words). Replace each word with the correct synonym. An example has been done.

concurrently	conversely	~~duration~~	format	intermediate
manual	medium	overlap	route	scenario
subordinate	team	temporarily	vision	

*Example: The total **time** of the project is expected to be two weeks.* __*duration*__

a) In a closed circulatory system, blood flows from the heart around a circulatory **path**, before returning to the heart. ______________

b) When a product becomes more expensive, people buy less; **on the other hand**, when it is cheaper, people consume more. ______________

c) The most likely **situation** is that interest rates will increase, which in the long run will lead to lower economic growth. ______________

d) Although it was advertised as a managerial position, it was in fact a **less important** role, not much better than a secretarial position. __________

e) The company is looking for a leader with great **ability to plan for the future** to lead it in a new direction. ______________

f) The two courses ran **at the same time**, meaning she had to choose one of them and could not study both. ______________

g) Although there is some **common ground** between the two theories, overall they are quite different. ______________

h) Testing was suspended **for a short time** while the allegations of cheating were investigated. ______________

i) The Internet is a very different **means** of communication from the television. ______________

j) Advances in machinery reduced the need for **hand** labour, leading more people to seek work in urban areas. ______________

k) The course is set at **middle** level, meaning it would be too easy for advanced learners. ______________

l) They worked as a **group** on the project, diving up the tasks to ensure they could complete the project efficiently and on time. ____________

m) You should check the **layout** of the final draft before submitting, for example, size of margins, font and line spacing. ____________

Task 4: Collocations #1

Match the following adj+n/v+n combinations to form common collocations of AWL sublist 9 words.

ethical	portion
significant	findings
gain	dilemma
maximum	insight
mutual	data
preliminary	action
qualitative	duration
domestic	norm
cultural	trust
military	sphere

Task 5: Collocations #2

The following are some further adj+n/v+n collocations with some of the AWL sublist 9 words from Exercise 4. Identify which word matches each set of collocations, and add in the collocations from Exercise 4. An example has been done.

duration	ethical	insight	military
mutual	~~norm~~	qualitative	preliminary
portion	sphere		

Words which collocate	Additional word from Ex 4	AWL Sublist 9 word
social--	*cultural--*	*norm*
-- force, -- power, -- service		
private-- , public--		
-- analysis, -- approach, -- method, -- research, -- study		
-- recognition, -- support, -- understanding		
-- consideration, -- issue, -- principle, -- problem, -- question		
give -- (into), offer -- (into), provide -- (into)		
-- data, -- result		
long --, short --		
large --, small --		

Task 6: Word form #1

Complete the following sentences by changing the word form of the word(s) in brackets. An example has been done for you.

Example: The rotation of the Earth causes the equator to bulge, as a result of which the Earth is not exactly spherical (sphere).

a) The student ______________ (accommodate) has recently been renovated and is now much more comfortable.
b) The wing of a bat is ______________ (analogy) to the wing of an insect, although their evolutionary origins are very different.
c) The recent flooding was an ______________ (anticipate) event. It was not expected to happen, and they were not prepared for it.
d) The equipment was very ______________ (bulk) and difficult to move.
e) The two research groups were working on the same project at the same time, which looked like more than just a ______________ (coincide).
f) Those who knew him praised his ______________ (devote) to the civil rights movement.
g) Climate change is leading to increased levels of coastal ______________ (erode), which in turn is leading to loss of homes.
h) The ______________ (mediate) between the two sides led to an acceptable agreement.
i) Despite having great freedom of choice, there is much ______________ (passive) in how consumers choose new products.
j) The ______________ (relax) of the regulations did not lead to the expected increase in crime.
k) Although parents may sometimes want to hit their child, they should exercise ______________ (restrain), since such punishment is harmful.
l) The wall of the apparatus used several layers of hardened plastic to increase ______________ (rigid).
m) In addition to his main income, he also derived a ______________ (supplement) income from interest on savings.
n) The ______________ (unify) of East and West Germany is one of the defining moments of the late twentieth century.

Task 7: Word form #2

Change the following adjectives into the *opposite* form, and add them to the mind map below according to the prefix (*im-*, *in-* or *un-*) or suffix (*-less*) which is used. Be careful of spelling. An example has been done.
Note: words with an asterisk are from level 7.*

attainable	cease	coherent	compatible
confined	controversial	definite*	diminished
ethical	finite	founded	mature
~~visible~~*			

Now, use each word *once only* to complete the following sentences.

Example: X rays are <u>invisible</u> to the human eye.

a) His goal was _______________. He could never hope to reach it.
b) The research experiment was considered to be _______________ since it subjected animals to undue cruelty.
c) For some time after suffering a stroke his speech was _______________. No one could understand him.
d) His views were very _______________and raised no objections.
e) The number of possible sentences in any language is _______________, since words can be put together in endless combinations.

f) The controversial decision led to ________________debate at the meeting. It seemed that it would never end.

g) His suspicions were ________________. There was no evidence whatsoever.

h) The ________________young of most mammal species need to be looked after until they are old enough to fend for themselves.

i) His love of research was ________________despite his age and he still continued to conduct experiments regularly.

j) A(n) ________________number of people signed up for the study. The experimenters did not have a clear idea of how many there were.

k) Their joy at being awarded the research grant was ________________.

l) The two parts of the apparatus were ________________and would not fit together.

Academic Word List: Sublist 10

adjacent

[ədʒeɪsənt]

adj

1. near or close to but not necessarily touching. E.g.: **lands adjacent to the mountains**, **New York and adjacent cities**
2. having a common boundary or edge; touching. [Syn: *neighboring*, *abutting*, *adjoining*, *conterminous*, *contiguous*]

n (thing)	verb	adj	opposite
x	x	adjacent	x
n (person)	**verb forms**	**adv**	**other**
x	x	x	x

----

albeit

[ɔlbiɪt]

adv

1. although.

n (thing)	verb	adj	opposite
x	x	x	x
n (person)	**verb forms**	**adv**	**other**
x	x	albeit	x

assemble

[əsembəl]

verb

1. collect in one place. E.g.: **We assembled in the church basement** [Syn: *meet, gather, forgather, foregather*]
2. make by putting pieces together. [Syn: *piece, put together, set up, tack, tack together*]

n (thing)	**verb**	**adj**	**opposite**
assembly	assemble	x	x
n (person)	**verb forms**	**adv**	**other**
x	assembled assembles assembling	x	x

----

collapse

[kəlæps]

verb

1. fold or close up. E.g.: **collapse the music stand**
2. break down, literally or metaphorically. E.g.: **The wall collapsed, The business collapsed, The roof collapsed** [Syn: *fall in, cave in, give, give way, break, founder*]
3. lose significance, effectiveness, or value. E.g.: **The stock market collapsed**

noun

1. an abrupt failure of function or health.
2. a sudden large decline of business or the prices of stocks (especially one that causes additional failures). [Syn: *crash*]

n (thing)	**verb**	**adj**	**opposite**
collapse	collapse	collapsible	x
n (person)	**verb forms**	**adv**	**other**
x	collapsed collapses collapsing	x	x

colleague

[kɑlig]

noun

1. a person who is member of your class or profession. E.g.: **the surgeon consulted his colleagues** [Syn: *confrere*, *fellow*]
2. an associate you work with. [Syn: *co-worker*, *fellow worker*, *workfellow*]

n (thing)	**verb**	**adj**	**opposite**
x	x	x	x
n (person)	**verb forms**	**adv**	**other**
colleague	x	x	x

----

compile

[kəmpaɪl]

verb

1. get or gather together. [Syn: *roll up*, *collect*, *accumulate*, *pile up*, *amass*, *hoard*]
2. put together out of existing material. E.g.: **compile a list** [Syn: *compose*]

n (thing)	**verb**	**adj**	**opposite**
compilation	compile	x	x
n (person)	**verb forms**	**adv**	**other**
x	compiled compiles compiling	x	x

conceive

[kənsiv]

verb

1. have the idea for. E.g.: **He conceived of a robot that would help paralyzed patients, This library was well conceived** [Syn: *gestate, conceptualize, conceptualise*]
2. become pregnant; undergo conception. E.g.: **She cannot conceive, My daughter was conceived on Christmas Day**

n (thing)	**verb**	**adj**	**opposite**
x	conceive	conceivable	inconceivable inconceivably
n (person)	**verb forms**	**adv**	**other**
x	conceived conceives conceiving	conceivably	x

---

convince

[kənvɪns]

verb

1. make (someone) agree, understand, or realize the truth or validity of something. E.g.: **He had finally convinced several customers of the advantages of his product** [Syn: *convert, win over*]

n (thing)	**verb**	**adj**	**opposite**
x	convince	x	unconvinced
n (person)	**verb forms**	**adv**	**other**
x	convinced convinces convincing	convincingly	x

depress

[dɪpres]

verb

1. cause to drop or sink. E.g.: **The lack of rain had depressed the water level in the reservoir** [Syn: *lower*]
2. lower someone's spirits; make downhearted. E.g.: **These news depressed her** [Syn: *deject, cast down, get down, dismay, dispirit, demoralize, demoralise*]

n (thing)	verb	adj	opposite
depression	depress	depressed depressing	x
n (person)	**verb forms**	**adv**	**other**
x	depressed depresses depressing	x	x

----

encounter

[ɪnkaʊntɜr]

verb

1. come upon, as if by accident; meet with. [Syn: *find, happen, chance, bump*]
2. be beset by. [Syn: *run into*]

n (thing)	verb	adj	opposite
x	encounter	x	x
n (person)	**verb forms**	**adv**	**other**
x	encountered encountering encounters	x	x

<u>Collocations from the ACL</u>

v+n: encounter difficulties, encounter problems.

enormous

[ɪnɔrməs]

adj

1. extraordinarily large in size or extent or amount or power or degree. E.g.: **an enormous boulder, enormous expenses** [Syn: *tremendous*]

n (thing)	verb	adj	opposite
enormity	x	enormous	x
n (person)	**verb forms**	**adv**	**other**
x	x	enormously	x

Collocations from the ACL
adj+n: (an) enormous amount (of), enormous impact.

---

forthcoming

[fɔrθkʌmɪŋ]

adj

1. of the relatively near future. E.g.: **the forthcoming holidays** [Syn: *approaching, upcoming, coming*]
2. available when required or as promised. E.g.: **federal funds were not forthcoming**

n (thing)	verb	adj	opposite
x	x	forthcoming	x
n (person)	**verb forms**	**adv**	**other**
x	x	x	x

incline

[ɪnklaɪn]

verb

1. be at an angle. [Syn: *slope, pitch*]

noun

1. an inclined surface or roadway that moves traffic from one level to another. [Syn: *ramp*]

n (thing)	**verb**	**adj**	**opposite**
inclination incline	incline	inclined	x
n (person)	**verb forms**	**adv**	**other**
x	inclined inclines inclining	x	x

---

integrity

[ɪntegrəti]

noun

1. an unreduced or unbroken completeness or totality. [Syn: unity, wholeness]
2. moral soundness.

n (thing)	**verb**	**adj**	**opposite**
integrity	x	x	x
n (person)	**verb forms**	**adv**	**other**
x	x	x	x

intrinsic

[ɪntrɪnsɪk]

adj

1. belonging to a thing by its very nature. E.g.: **form was treated as something intrinsic, as the very essence of the thing- John Dewey** [Syn: *intrinsical*]

n (thing)	verb	adj	opposite
x	x	intrinsic	x
n (person)	**verb forms**	**adv**	**other**
x	x	intrinsically	x

---

invoke

[ɪnvoʊk]

verb

1. request earnestly (something from somebody); ask for aid or protection. [Syn: *appeal*]
2. cite as an authority; resort to. E.g.: **He invoked the law that would save him**, **She invoked an ancient law** [Syn: *appeal*]

n (thing)	verb	adj	opposite
x	invoke	x	x
n (person)	**verb forms**	**adv**	**other**
x	invoked invokes invoking	x	x

levy

[levi]

verb

1. impose and collect. E.g.: **levy a fine** [Syn: *impose*]

noun

1. a charge imposed and collected.

n (thing)	verb	adj	opposite
levy	levy	x	x
n (person)	**verb forms**	**adv**	**other**
x	x	x	x

----

likewise

[laɪkwaɪz]

adv

1. in like or similar manner. E.g.: **some people have little power to do good, and have likewise little strength to resist evil- Samuel Johnson** [Syn: *similarly*]

n (thing)	verb	adj	opposite
x	x	x	x
n (person)	**verb forms**	**adv**	**other**
x	x	likewise	x

nonetheless

[nʌnðəles]

adv

1. despite anything to the contrary (usually following a concession). [Syn: *however, nevertheless, withal, still, yet, all the same, even so, notwithstanding*]

n (thing)	verb	adj	opposite
x	x	x	x
n (person)	**verb forms**	**adv**	**other**
x	x	nonetheless	x

---

notwithstanding

[natwɪ θ stændɪŋ]

adv

1. despite anything to the contrary (usually following a concession). [Syn: *however, nevertheless, withal, still, yet, all the same, even so, nonetheless*]

n (thing)	verb	adj	opposite
x	x	x	x
n (person)	**verb forms**	**adv**	**other**
x	x	notwithstanding	x

odd

[ɑd]

adj

1. not divisible by two.
2. not easily explained. E.g.: **it is odd that his name is never mentioned**

n (thing)	verb	adj	opposite
odds	x	odd	x
n (person)	**verb forms**	**adv**	**other**
x	x	x	x

---

ongoing

[ɑngoʊɪŋ]

adj

1. currently happening. E.g.: **an ongoing economic crisis** [Syn: *in progress*]

n (thing)	verb	adj	opposite
x	x	ongoing	x
n (person)	**verb forms**	**adv**	**other**
x	x	x	x

Collocations from the ACL

adj+n: ongoing debate, ongoing process.

panel

[pænəl]

verb

1. decorate with panels. E.g.: **panel the walls with wood**

noun

1. a group of people gathered for a special purpose as to plan or discuss an issue or judge a contest etc.
2. a committee appointed to judge a competition. [Syn: *jury*]
3. sheet that forms a distinct (usually flat) section or component of something.

n (thing)	**verb**	**adj**	**opposite**
panel	panel	x	x
n (person)	**verb forms**	**adv**	**other**
x	panelled panelling panels	x	x

---

persist

[pɜrsɪst]

verb

1. continue to exist. [Syn: *prevail*, *die hard*, *run*, *endure*]
2. be persistent, refuse to stop. E.g.: **he persisted to call me every night, The child persisted and kept asking questions** [Syn: *persevere*, *hang in*, *hang on*, *hold on*]

n (thing)	**verb**	**adj**	**opposite**
persistence	persist	persistent persisting	x
n (person)	**verb forms**	**adv**	**other**
x	persisted persisting persists	persistently	x

pose

[poʊz]

verb

1. introduce. E.g.: **This poses an interesting question** [Syn: *present*]

n (thing)	verb	adj	opposite
x	pose	x	x
n (person)	**verb forms**	**adv**	**other**
x	posed poses posing	x	x

Collocations from the ACL

v+n: pose (a) challenge, pose (a) problem, pose (a) question, pose (a) threat (to).

---

reluctance

[rɪlʌktəns]

noun

1. a certain degree of unwillingness. E.g.: **a reluctance to commit himself** [Syn: *hesitancy*, *hesitation*, *disinclination*, *indisposition*]

n (thing)	verb	adj	opposite
reluctance	x	reluctant	x
n (person)	**verb forms**	**adv**	**other**
x	x	reluctantly	x

so-called

[soʊkɔld]

adj

1. doubtful or suspect. E.g.: **these so-called experts are no help** [Syn: *alleged*, *supposed*]

n (thing)	**verb**	**adj**	**opposite**
x	x	so-called	x
n (person)	**verb forms**	**adv**	**other**
x	x	x	x

---

straightforward

[streɪtfɔrwɜrd]

adj

1. free from ambiguity. E.g.: **a straightforward set of instructions**

n (thing)	**verb**	**adj**	**opposite**
x	x	straightforward	x
n (person)	**verb forms**	**adv**	**other**
x	x	x	x

Collocations from the ACL

adv+adj: fairly straightforward, relatively straightforward.

undergo

[ʌndɜrgoʊ]

verb

1. (of mental or physical states or experiences) experience or feel. E.g.: **undergo a strange sensation, The chemical undergoes a sudden change** [Syn: *experience, receive, have, get*]

n (thing)	**verb**	**adj**	**opposite**
x	undergo	x	x
n (person)	**verb forms**	**adv**	**other**
x	undergoes undergoing undergone underwent	x	x

---

whereby

[werbaɪ]

adv

1. by or through which. E.g.: **the means whereby we achieved our goal**
2. as a result of which.

n (thing)	**verb**	**adj**	**opposite**
x	x	x	x
n (person)	**verb forms**	**adv**	**other**
x	x	whereby	x

Exercises (Sublist 10)

Task 1: Focus on Meaning #1

Study the following text on **Stressors**. Fill in the gaps using words from the box. All are words from AWL sublist 10. [Note: words from sublist 7 (underlined), sublist 8 (*italics*) and sublist 9 (**bold**) are also shown, for review/preview purposes.]

colleagues	depression	encounter	likewise
ongoing	persist	pose	undergoing

Stressors, the stimuli that initiate the stress process, can be placed into one of two broad categories: chronic and acute. Chronic stressors include events that _____________ over an extended period of time, such as caring for a parent with dementia, long-term unemployment, or imprisonment. Acute stressors involve brief focal events that sometimes continue to be experienced as overwhelming well after the event has ended, such as falling on an icy sidewalk and breaking your leg (Cohen, Janicki-Deverts, & Miller, 2007). Potential stressors include major traumatic events, significant life changes, daily hassles, as well as other situations in which a person is regularly exposed to threat, challenge, or danger.

Some stressors involve traumatic events or situations in which a person is exposed to actual or threatened death or serious injury. Stressors in this category include exposure to **military** combat, threatened or actual physical assaults (e.g., physical attacks, sexual assault, robbery, childhood abuse), terrorist attacks, natural disasters (e.g., earthquakes, floods, hurricanes), _____________ major surgery, and automobile accidents.

Most stressors that we _____________ are not nearly as *intense* as the ones described above. Many potential stressors we face involve events or situations that require us to make changes in our _____________ lives and require time as we adjust to those changes. Examples include death of a close family member, marriage, divorce, moving, and starting a new job. This kind of stress can be both positive and negative. However, most of the available evidence suggests that, at least as far as mental health is concerned, undesirable or negative events are more strongly associated with poor outcomes (such as _____________) than are desirable, positive events (Hatch & Dohrenwend, 2007).

Potential stressors do not always involve major life events. Daily hassles—the minor irritations and annoyances that are part of our everyday lives (e.g., rush hour traffic, lost keys, unfriendly _____________, inclement weather, arguments with friends or family)—can build on one another and leave us just as stressed as life change events (Kanner, Coyne, Schaefer, & Lazarus, 1981).

Stressors can include situations in which one is frequently exposed to challenging and unpleasant events, such as difficult, demanding, or unsafe working conditions. Although most jobs and occupations can at times be demanding, some are clearly more stressful than others. For example, most people would likely agree that a firefighter's work is **inherently** more stressful than that of a florist. _____________, most would agree that jobs containing various unpleasant elements, such as those requiring exposure to loud noise (heavy equipment operator), those which _____________ a danger to health (healthcare worker during a contagious pandemic), those involving constant harassment and threats of physical violence (prison guard) or perpetual frustration (bus driver in a major city), or those mandating that an employee work alternating day and night shifts (hotel desk clerk), are much more demanding—and thus, more stressful—than those that do not contain such elements.

Adapted from Psychology, 1, Chapter 14 | Stress, Lifestyle, and Health © 2017 Rice University. Download for free at https://openstax.org/details/books/psychology.

Task 2: Focus on Meaning #2

The following sentences each contain an underlined word, which can be replaced by a synonym from the box below (all sublist 10 words). Replace each word with the correct synonym. An example has been done.

adjacent	albeit	collapse	~~enormous~~	forthcoming
integrity	intrinsic	invoke	levy	nonetheless
notwithstanding	odd	panel	so-called	whereby

*Example: Although case studies provide a **huge** amount of information, they are very specific and it may be difficult to apply what is learned to the general population.* ___*enormous*___

a) Productivity in the country has increased steadily over the past three decades, **in spite of** the current global recession. _______________

b) Local governments can **impose** their own taxes on local businesses and individuals. _______________

c) Many **supposed** charities are in fact nothing of the kind, and are making considerable profits for their board members. _______________

d) The government has brought in legislation **so that** revenue from ecotourism can be used directly to preserve the environment visited by tourists. _______________

e) There has been considerable increase economic growth over the past three years, **although** at a slower rate than experts predicted. _______________

f) In social science experiments it is sometimes necessary to mislead participants in order to maintain the **soundness** of the experiment. _______________

g) In economics, fiat money has no **basic** value, but is declared by a government to be the legal tender of a country. _______________

h) The somatosensory cortex of the brain is organized topographically, meaning, for example, that part of the cortex that processes information from the hand is **next** to the part that processes information from the wrist. _______________

i) The **soon-to-be published** article on the results of the Covid-19 vaccine is eagerly awaited by government health officials. _______________

j) The judge chose to **use** the law protecting refugees from being exported back to their own country. _______________

k) Although the drug led to a reduction of symptoms in a majority of patients, it was a failure **anyway**, since it had too many side effects. _______________

l) Due to his expertise in the field, the professor was invited to be part of a **committee** of climate change experts presenting information to businesses. _______________

m) Although many people hold beliefs that can be considered **strange**, this is different from a delusion, which is a belief that is clearly absurd. _______________

n) There were many reasons for the **fall** of communist governments at the end of the Cold War. _______________

Task 3: Collocations

Match the following combinations to form common collocations of AWL

encounter	debate/process
enormous	straightforward
fairly/relatively	a challenge/a problem/a question/a threat to
ongoing	difficulties/problems
pose	amount of/impact

Now use **one** collocation from the above list to complete the following sentences. Note: sometimes more than one answer is possible.

a) The rise of armed conflict in the region will ________________________ to travellers, who should only go there if absolutely essential.
b) Learning to ride a bicycle is a ________________________ task.
c) His research had a(n) ______________________ on future researchers in the field.
d) Many beginning academic writers _____________________ with collocation use.
e) There is a(n) ________________________ about whether soft drugs such as marijuana should be legalised.

Task 4: Word form

Complete the following sentences by changing the word form of the word(s) in brackets. An example has been done for you.

Example: Several different criminal charges were levied (levy) against them.

a) After the precautions they took to ensure accurate measurements, a large margin of error was _______________ (conceive).
b) The respondents had an _______________ (incline) to agree with each other when questioned in pairs.
c) Although the report claimed to present new information, it was in fact a _______________ (compile) of previous, much older research data.
d) They waited for the _______________ (assemble) of all the participants before they began the meeting.
e) His arguments were _______________ (convince), which meant that nobody believed his theory to be correct.
f) He was ___________ (reluctance) to release the results until the trial was complete.
g) One of the effects of prolonged stress is _______________ (depress).
h) Some students give up too easily, and teachers should communicate to them the importance of _______________ (persist) in learning.
i) He _______________ (undergo) brain surgery last week in an effort to remove the tumour, though it is unclear if the operation was successful.
k) The did not fully understand the _______________ (enormous) of the task until they had started, when they realized just how difficult it would be.

Answers to exercises

Sublist 7

Task 1: Focus on Meaning #1

Energy is an important element at all levels of society. We live in a very interdependent world, and access to adequate and reliable energy resources is *crucial* for economic growth and for maintaining the quality of our lives. There are two major types of energy sources: renewable and non-renewable. Renewable sources are energy sources that are replenished through naturally occurring, **ongoing** processes, on a time scale that is much shorter than the **anticipated** lifetime of the civilization using the source, making them almost **infinite**. Non-renewable sources are depleted once some of the energy they contain is **extracted** and transformed into other kinds of energy, which means they are **finite**. The natural processes by which non-renewable sources are formed typically take place over geological time scales.

Our most important non-renewable energy sources are fossil fuels, such as coal, petroleum, and natural gas. These account for 81% of the world's energy consumption. Burning fossil fuels creates **chemical** reactions that transform potential energy, in the molecular structures of the reactants, into thermal energy and products. This thermal energy can be used to heat buildings or to operate steam-driven machinery. Electrical power generation is mostly derived from transferring energy in expanding steam, *via* turbines, into mechanical work, which rotates coils of wire in magnetic fields to generate electricity.

Nuclear energy is the other non-renewable source and supplies about 3% of the world's consumption. *Nuclear* reactions generate energy by transforming potential energy, in the structure of nuclei, into thermal energy. The thermal energy obtained from *nuclear* reactions can be transferred into other forms in the same ways that energy from fossil fuels are used.

An unfortunate byproduct of relying on energy produced from the combustion of fossil fuels is the **release** of carbon dioxide into the atmosphere and its contribution to **global** warming. *Nuclear* energy ***poses*** environmental problems as well, including the safety and **disposal** of *nuclear* waste. Besides these important consequences, reserves of non-renewable sources of energy are limited and, given the rapidly growing rate of world energy consumption, may not last for more than a few hundred years. Some estimate that oil reserves will be exhausted within mere **decades**.

Four renewable energy sources which involve quite different types of energy transformations from those just discussed are hydropower, wind power, geothermal power, and solar power.

Hydropower is produced by the **conversion** of the gravitational potential energy of falling or flowing water into kinetic energy and then into work to run electric generators or machinery. Wats to harness the mechanical energy in ocean surface waves and tides is in development.

Wind power also **converts** kinetic energy into work, which can be used directly to generate electricity, operate mills, and propel sailboats.

The interior of Earth has a great deal of thermal energy, part of which is left over from its original formation and part of which is **released** from radioactive minerals (a form of natural *nuclear* energy). It will take a very long time for this geothermal energy to escape into space, so people generally regard it as a renewable source, when actually, it is just inexhaustible on human time scales.

The source of solar power is energy carried by the electromagnetic waves radiated by the Sun. Most of this energy is carried by **visible** light and infrared (heat) radiation. When suitable materials absorb electromagnetic waves, radiant energy is **converted** into thermal energy, which can be used to heat water, or when concentrated, to make steam and generate electricity. However, another way to generate energy from sunlight is *via* photovoltaics (PV), which are **comprised** of semi-conductor materials such as silicon which produce electricity directly using what is known as the photoelectric effect.

Task 2: Focus on Meaning #2

Matter is defined as anything that occupies space and has mass, and it is all around us. Solids and liquids are more obviously matter: We can see that they take up space, and their weight tells us that they have mass. Gases are also matter; if gases did not take up space, a balloon would not inflate (increase its volume) when filled with gas.

Solids, liquids, and gases are the three states of matter commonly found on earth. A solid is **rigid** and possesses a **definite** shape. A liquid flows and takes the shape of its container, except that it forms a flat or slightly curved upper surface when acted upon by gravity, a **phenomenon** which does not happen in space (in zero gravity, liquids assume a **spherical** shape). Both liquid and solid samples have volumes that are very nearly independent of pressure. A gas takes both the shape and volume of its container.

A **comprehensive** classification of matter should include a fourth state, plasma, which occurs naturally in the interiors of stars. A plasma is a gaseous state of matter that contains *appreciable* numbers of electrically charged particles. The presence of these charged particles imparts **unique** properties to plasmas that **differentiate** them from gases and justify their classification as a distinct state of matter. In addition to stars, plasmas are found in some other high-temperature environments, both natural and man-made, such as lightning strikes and certain television screens.

Some samples of matter appear to have properties of solids, liquids, and/or gases at the same time. This can occur when the sample is composed of many small pieces, for example sand, which can be poured in an **identical** way to how a liquid is poured because it is composed of many small grains of solid sand. Matter can also have properties of more than one state when it is a mixture, such as with clouds. Clouds appear to behave **somewhat** like gases, though they are actually mixtures of air (gas) and tiny particles of water (liquid or solid).

Task 3: Focus on Meaning #3

a) Although each half of the brain is associated with certain functions, both areas interact to provide the **basis** for our thoughts and behaviours.__foundation__

b) Military expenditure, **combined** with a decrease in tax revenue, have been the main contributors to the growing budget deficit.__coupled__

c) In Douglas McGregor's classification, Theory X managers believe that people are **only** motivated by money.__solely__

d) Access to financial capital helps a business to make physical capital investments, and, **in the end**, can lead to job creation.__ultimately__

e) A peer-reviewed journal article is read by several other experts in the same field to provide feedback about the quality of the article before it is accepted for **printing**.__publication__

f) Beliefs about racial differences and performance levels of athletes persist despite a number of examples to the **opposite**.__contrary

g) The informed consent form will provide participants with a **certainty** that any data collected in the experiment will remain confidential.__guarantee__

h) Scholars in each of the three major **perspectives** of sociology would view the topic in a different way.__paradigms__

i) The primary **means** of communication for deaf people is sign language.__mode__

j) It took a long time to find the book in the library as it had been **placed** in the Child Psychology section rather than in the Adult Psychology section.__filed__

k) Lack of parental discipline can be associated with lower **scores** in school.__grades__

l) The teacher disagreed with his **viewpoint** that all people are lazy.__thesis__

Task 4: Collocations #1

The following are the collocations:

classic example, cultural phenomenon, high priority, infinite number, political ideology, popular media, *recent decades*, transmit data

The following shows the pairs as per the exercise in the book:

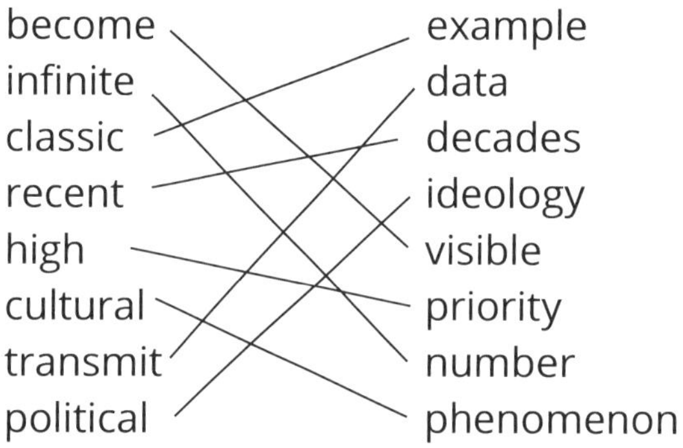

Task 5: Collocations #2

key --, related --, cover (a) --, discuss (a) --	**topic**
-- individual, -- opportunity, -- position	**unique**
digital --, electronic --, global --, national --, popular --, visual --	**media**
-- account, -- approach, -- overview, -- review, -- system	**comprehensive**
next --, previous --, early --.	**decade(s)**
-- capitalism, -- context, -- culture, -- economy, -- issue, -- market, -- marketplace, -- media, -- network, -- perspective, -- shift, -- structure, -- trade, -- village	**global**
-- equilibrium, -- nature, -- process, -- system	**dynamic**
-- data, -- information	**extract**
-- data, -- evidence, -- investigation, -- research, -- study, -- support, -- work	**empirical**

Task 6: Word form #1

a) There were many **volunteers** (voluntary) who assisted the hospital during the Covid-19 crisis.

b) His qualities as a great leader were **undeniable** (deny). There was no one who disagreed.

c) The reckless action of the president was halted by the **intervention** (intervene) of his chief of staff.

d) The psychological problems which children suffer from will often persist into **adulthood** (adult).

e) Scientists are working on increasingly **innovative** (innovate) solutions to the energy crisis.

f) Most adults are more interested in intimacy than in **isolation** (isolate) from others.

g) The cost of the treatment was **prohibitive** (prohibit), which led to the company discontinuing its research in the area.

h) The company operated on a very **hierarchical** (hierarchy) system, and employees could not communicate above their immediate supervisor.

i) Many believe that the sacrifice made by Coretta Scott King, Martin Luther King's wife, **aided** (aid) his success.

j) The company **channelled** (channel) most information for the public through its official website.

k) Some psychologists employ virtual reality therapy to give patients a **simulation** (simulate) and so help them overcome their fears.

l) It is important to use **quotation** (quote) marks, along with an in-text citation, when copying someone’s exact words into your text.

Task 7: Word form #2

adapt	adaptability / adaptation
advocate	advocacy
confirm	confirmation
convert	conversion
deny	*denial*
dispose	disposal
eliminate	elimination
equip	equipment
extract	extract / extraction
infer	inference
innovate	innovation
insert	insert / insertion
prioritise	priority / prioritisation
quote	quote / quotation
reverse	reverse / reversal
submit	submission
successor	succession
survive	survival
transmit	transmission
unique	uniqueness
visible	visibility

-al	-ance/ -ence	-cy	-bility	-ment	-rsion	*Same as v/adj form*
denial disposal reversal survival	inference	advocacy	visibility adaptability	equipment	conversion	extract insert quote reverse
			-ity	**-ness**	**-ssion**	**-tion**
			priority	uniqueness	submission succession transmission	adaptation confirmation elimination extraction innovation insertion prioritisation quotation

Sublist 8

Task 1: Focus on Meaning #1

Markets that allow personal and business rewards and incentives for increasing human and physical capital encourage overall macroeconomic growth. For example, workers have an incentive to acquire additional human capital, because additional education and skills give them the **prospect** of higher wages. Firms have an incentive to invest in physical capital and in training workers, because this is usually **accompanied** by higher profits in the long run. Both individuals and firms seek to **exploit** new technologies, because even small inventions can make work easier or lead to product improvement. Much of the rapid growth since the late nineteenth century has come from harnessing the power of competitive markets to allocate resources. This market orientation typically reaches beyond national borders and includes openness to international trade.

Despite a general market orientation, there remain **crucial** roles for government to play. One of these is to correct failures in how capital and technology are allocated. In addition, government can guide or influence markets toward certain outcomes. The following examples **highlight** some important areas that governments around the world have chosen to invest in to facilitate economic growth.

- The Danish government requires all children under 16 to attend school. They can choose to attend a public school (Folkeskole) or a private school. Students do not pay tuition to attend Folkeskole. Although primary/secondary (elementary/high) schools are **predominantly** public schools (87%), the private sector is growing, and one way the government encourages this is to supply vouchers to citizens who choose private school.
- In the United States, as in other countries, private investment is taxed. Low taxes encourage investment, and by choosing to **minimise** tax revenue in the private investment area, the government can encourage greater economic growth.
- The Japanese government in the mid-1990s undertook significant **infrastructure** projects to improve roads and public works. This in turn increased the stock of physical capital and ultimately economic growth.
- The island of Mauritius is one of the few African nations to encourage international trade in government-supported Special Economic Zones. Special Economic Zones (SEZ) **denote** areas of the country, usually with access to a port where, among other benefits, the government does not tax sales, **thereby** encouraging trade and allowing businesses to be more profitable. As a result of its SEZ status, Mauritius has enjoyed above-average economic growth since the 1980s.
- The European Union has strong programs to invest in scientific research. Firms which received support from their government increased their research

intensity and had more sales. Governments can support scientific research and technical training that helps to create and spread new technologies. They can also help inventors profit from their inventions **via** legal measures such as protection of intellectual property rights.

Task 2: Focus on Meaning #2

The continued protests during meetings of the World Trade Organization, the World Bank and the International Monetary Fund show that many people in **contemporary** society still fear world trade and globalization. While there are some definite disadvantages to globalization, most economists would agree that these are more than **offset** by the positives of the trend towards global trade.

The negatives of global trade include jobs lost due to imports or production shifting abroad, the fear of jobs being lost in this way, and the threat of companies exporting jobs if workers do not accept pay cuts. Sending domestic jobs to another country is called outsourcing. Many U.S. companies, such as Dell, IBM, and AT&T, have set up call service centers in India, the Philippines, and other countries. The practice of outsourcing is increasingly **widespread**, with even engineering and research and development jobs being outsourced. Outsourcing and "American jobs" were a big part of the 2016 presidential election, won by Donald Trump.

A closer look reveals that globalization has been the engine that creates jobs and wealth. The following are some of the main **pluses** of global trade.

- Productivity grows more quickly when countries produce goods and services in which they have a comparative advantage, allowing living standards to increase.
- Global competition and importing cheap **commodities** keep prices down, so inflation is less likely to stop economic growth. However, in some cases this is not working because countries **manipulate** the value of their **currency** to get a price advantage.
- An open economy spurs innovation with fresh ideas from abroad.
- Through infusion of foreign capital and technology, global trade provides poor countries with the chance to develop economically by spreading prosperity, although this does not always happen evenly, with more prosperous members of society tending to **accumulate** wealth more rapidly than the less prosperous.
- More information is shared between two trading partners that may not have much in common initially, including **insight** into local cultures and customs, which may help the two nations expand their collective knowledge and learn ways to compete globally.

In short, while there will **inevitably** be some disagreement over whether globalization is a positive trend, most economists **appreciate** that, on balance, the advantages outweigh the drawbacks.

Task 3: Focus on Meaning #3

a) In economic theory, supply is limited, since resources are limited, whereas demand is **almost** unlimited.__virtually__

b) A copy of the consent form used in the survey is given in the **additional sections** at the end of the report.__appendices__

c) A plot of the results is shown in the two **diagrams** on the following page.__charts__

d) Although the report did not directly accuse the manager of wrongdoing, there was **indirect** criticism of the way he acted.__implicit__

e) Before becoming chair of the genetics department, he was a medical **expert** in the specialising in viruses.__practitioner__

f) The average U.S. household spends roughly one-third of its income on food and **car** expenses.__vehicle__

g) Advances in technology will **in the end** lead to the loss of more manual jobs.__inevitably__

h) The earlier hypothesis was **discarded** when two experiments failed to find supporting data.__abandoned__

i) When conducting experiments involving people, ethical **recommendations** need to be followed very closely.__guidelines__

j) Failure to deliver the good on time led to the **ending** of the contract.__termination__

k) An academic essay requires you to organise your writing into separate **passages**, each of which should contain a clear topic and supporting ideas.__paragraphs__

Task 4: Collocations #1

The following are the collocations:

change dramatically, dramatic increase, economic exploitation, intensive study, nuclear energy, revised edition, single currency

The following shows the pairs as per the exercise in the book.

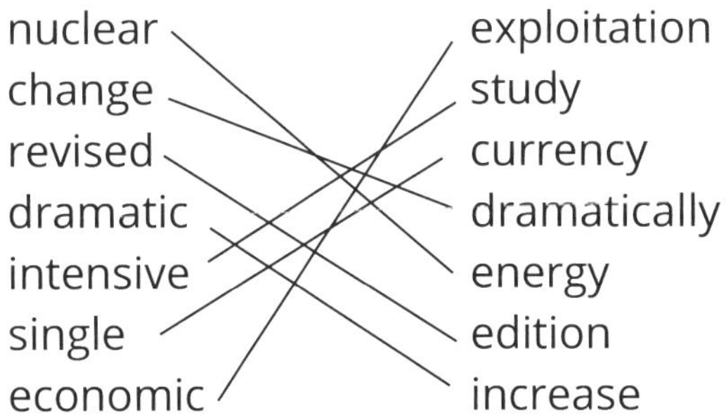

Task 5: Collocations #2

a) Although considered unsafe by some, **nuclear** ~~family~~/**power**/~~war~~/~~weapon~~ is a safe and reliable way to generate electricity for homes.

b) The idea that the colonization of Africa was a necessary evil is a ~~central~~/~~key~~/~~major~~/**recurrent theme** in his writing. It appears in almost all of his books.

c) Despite their **radical** ~~changes~~/~~critiques~~/**differences**/~~transformations~~ on many issues, the two scholars managed to agree on an overall approach.

d) Safety with chemicals and apparatus is a **crucial** ~~difference~~/**factor**/~~importance~~/~~question~~ if any scientific experiment.

e) Gun control is a **contemporary** ~~debate~~/**issue**/~~life~~/society that divides many people in the United States.

f) Fluctuations in the temperature during the experiment led to a significant **random error**/~~sample~~/~~variable~~ in the measurements.

g) There is **widespread** ~~acceptance~~/~~belief~~/**support**/~~use~~ for stronger environmental powers by local governments.

h) Television is the most common form of **visual** ~~image~~/**media**/~~perception~~/~~representation~~ in our everyday lives.

Task 6: Word form #1

a) Employees will be automatically (automate) enrolled in the scheme unless they voluntarily opt out.

b) He was chosen to resolve the dispute since he was completely unbiased (bias). He did not have any reason to favour either side.

c) The two methods were complementary (complement) and combined together to enable greater accuracy in measuring results.

d) Since the two sets of results were contradictory (contradict), a third experiment was conducted to see which set were valid.

e) The metal detector (detect) aided in the discovery of Saxon treasure at the site.

f) Managers need to monitor the implementation of a plan and make corrections to any deviations (deviate) in the plan.

g) Children in the group under study were rewarded when they exhibited (exhibit) positive behaviour.

h) Errors in measurement were likely the result of fluctuations (fluctuate) in the temperature.
i) All of the new staff members were required to attend the induction (induce) events in the first week.
j) The safety inspectors (inspect) decided that the building was unfit for use. They ordered it to be closed down.
k) The restoration (restore) of the public hall damaged by fire was proceeding as planned.
l) Since fewer than half of the members were present for the meeting, they decided to reschedule (schedule).

Task 7: Word form #2

These are the noun forms.

ambiguity	arbitrariness	clarity	conformity
displacement	dramatisation	~~eventuality~~	intensity
randomness	reinforcement	revision	tension
uniformity	visualisation		

These are the noun forms on the suffix mind map.

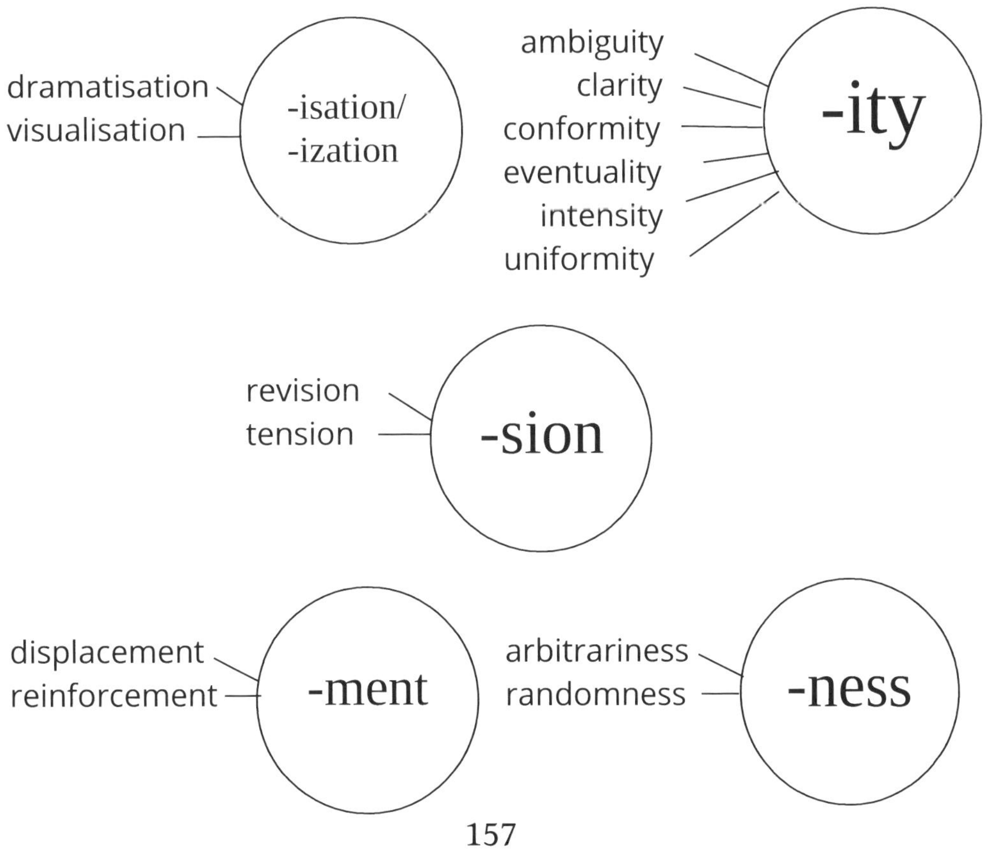

Sublist 9

Task 1: Focus on Meaning #1

It was not until the late nineteenth century that medical researchers discovered non-surgical methods to look inside the living body. The first of these techniques was the X-ray, a form of high energy electromagnetic radiation with a short wavelength capable of penetrating solids and ionizing gases. X-rays are best used to *visualize* hard body structures such as teeth and bones. Like many forms of high energy radiation, however, X-rays are capable of damaging cells and initiating changes that can lead to cancer. This danger of excessive exposure to X-rays was not fully *appreciated* for many years after their *widespread* use. **Refinements** and enhancements of X-ray techniques have continued throughout the twentieth and twenty-first centuries, and effective shielding and limiting exposure mean the danger of irradiation to the patient and the operator is now **minimal**.

X-rays can depict a two-dimensional image of a body region, and only from a single angle. In contrast, more recent medical imaging technologies produce data that is integrated and analyzed by computers to produce three-dimensional images or images that reveal aspects of body functioning. The main ones are: computed tomography; magnetic resonance imaging; positron emission tomography; and ultrasonography.

Tomography refers to imaging by sections. Computed tomography (CT) is a noninvasive imaging technique that uses computers to analyze several cross-sectional X-rays in order to reveal minute details about structures in the body. Invented in the 1970s, CT scanning is routine for many types of diagnostic evaluations. Its level of detail is so precise that it can allow physicians to measure the size of a mass down to a millimeter. The main disadvantage of CT scanning is that it exposes patients to a dose of radiation many times higher than that of X-rays. In fact, children who ***undergo*** CT scans are at increased risk of developing cancer, as are adults who have multiple CT scans.

Magnetic resonance imaging (MRI) is a noninvasive medical imaging technique based on an **inherent** property of matter, discovered by *nuclear* physicists in the 1930s, which is that when matter is exposed to magnetic fields and radio waves, it emits radio signals. In 1970, a physician and researcher named Raymond Damadian noticed that malignant (cancerous) tissue gave off different signals than normal body tissue. He applied for a patent for the first MRI scanning **device**, which was in use clinically by the early 1980s. MRI allows for precise imaging, and is especially useful in discovering tumours. MRI has the major advantage of not exposing patients to radiation. Drawbacks of MRI scans include their much higher cost, and patient discomfort with the procedure. The MRI scanner subjects the patient to such powerful electromagnets that the scan room must be shielded, and the patient must be enclosed in a metal tube-like scanner for the **duration** of the scan, sometimes as long as thirty minutes. Being **confined** in such a small space can be uncomfortable and impractical for ill patients. The scanner is also extremely noisy, which can **trigger** anxiety or fear in patients. These problems have been overcome somewhat with the development of "open" MRI scanning, which does not require the patient to be entirely enclosed in the metal tube.

Positron emission tomography (PET) is a medical imaging technique involving the use of ***so-called*** radiopharmaceuticals, substances that emit radiation that is short-lived and therefore relatively safe to administer to the body. Although the first PET scanner was introduced in 1961, it took 15 more years before radiopharmaceuticals were combined with the technique and **revolutionized** its potential. The main advantage is that PET can illustrate physiologic activity of the organ or organs being targeted, including nutrient metabolism and blood flow, whereas CT and MRI scans can only show static images. PET is widely used to diagnose a multitude of conditions, such as heart disease, the spread of cancer, certain forms of infection, brain abnormalities, bone disease, and thyroid disease.

Ultrasonography is an imaging technique that uses the transmission of high-frequency sound waves into the body to generate an echo signal that is converted by a computer into a real-time image of anatomy and physiology. Ultrasonography is the least invasive of all imaging techniques, and it is therefore used more freely in sensitive situations such as pregnancy. The main disadvantages of ultrasonography are that the image quality is heavily operator-dependent and that it is unable to penetrate bone and gas.

Task 2: Focus on Meaning #2

Today, scientists agree that good research is **ethical** in nature and is guided by a basic respect for human dignity and safety. However, this has not always been the case. Modern researchers must demonstrate that the research they perform is **ethically** sound.

RESEARCH INVOLVING HUMAN PARTICIPANTS
Any experiment involving the participation of human subjects is governed by extensive, strict **guidelines** designed to ensure that the experiment does not result in harm. Any research institution that receives federal support for research involving human participants must have access to an institutional review board (IRB). The IRB is a committee of individuals often made up of members of the institution's administration, scientists, and community members. The purpose of the IRB is to review proposals for research that involves human participants, and approval from the IRB is required before any such experiment can **commence**.

One **integral** component of any experiment approved by an institution's IRB is an informed consent form, which must be signed by each participant before they can take part in the experiment. An informed consent form provides a written description of what participants can expect during the experiment, including potential risks and implications of the research. It also gives **assurances** about the voluntary nature of the research, and confidentiality of data collection. In cases where research participants are under the age of 18, the parents or legal guardians are required to sign the form on **behalf** of their child.

Pioneer German sociologist Max Weber (1864–1920) identified another **crucial** **ethical** concern. Social science research often uses **qualitative** data, for example from case studies or ethnographies, rather than statistical data. Weber stated that researchers must remain impartial or 'value neutral', without **bias** or judgment, during the course of a study and when interpreting and publishing results. They are obligated to disclose research findings and should not omit or **distort** significant data. Many researchers believe, however, that it is impossible to set aside personal values and retain complete objectivity. They caution readers, rather, to understand that social science studies may, by necessity, contain a certain amount of value **bias**. It does not discredit the results but allows readers to view them as one form of truth rather than a singular fact.

RESEARCH INVOLVING ANIMAL SUBJECTS

Many psychologists conduct research involving animal subjects. Often, these researchers use rodents or birds as the subjects of their experiments; the APA estimates that 90% of all animal research in psychology uses these species (American Psychological Association, n.d.). Because many basic processes in animals are sufficiently similar to those in humans, these animals are acceptable substitutes for research that would be considered **unethical** in human participants.

This does not mean that animal researchers are immune to **ethical** concerns. Indeed, the humane treatment of animal research subjects is a critical aspect of this type of research. Researchers must design their experiments to **minimize** any pain or distress experienced by animals serving as research subjects.

Whereas IRBs review research proposals that involve human participants, animal experimental proposals are reviewed by an Institutional Animal Care and Use Committee (IACUC). An IACUC consists of institutional administrators, scientists, veterinarians, and community members. This committee is charged with ensuring that all experimental proposals require the humane treatment of animal research subjects. It also conducts semi-annual **inspections** of all animal facilities to ensure that the research **protocols** are being followed, and has the power to **suspend** or halt any experiments which **violate** its regulations. No animal research project can proceed without the committee's approval.

Task 3: Focus on Meaning #3

a) In a closed circulatory system, blood flows from the heart around a circulatory **path**, before returning to the heart.__route__

b) When a product becomes more expensive, people buy less; **on the other hand**, when it is cheaper, people consume more.__conversely__

c) The most likely **situation** is that interest rates will increase, which in the long run will lead to lower economic growth.__scenario__

d) Although it was advertised as a managerial position, it was in fact a **less important** role, not much better than a secretarial position.__subordinate__

e) The company is looking for a leader with great **ability to plan for the future** to lead it in a new direction.__vision__

f) The two courses ran **at the same time**, meaning she had to choose one of them and could not study both.__concurrently__

g) Although there is some **common ground** between the two theories, overall they are quite different.__overlap__

h) Testing was suspended **for a short time** while the allegations of cheating were investigated.__temporarily__

i) The Internet is a very different **means** of communication from the television.__medium__

j) Advances in machinery reduced the need for **hand** labour, leading more people to seek work in urban areas.__manual__

k) The course is set at **middle** level, meaning it would be too easy for advanced learners.__intermediate__

l) They worked as a **group** on the project, diving up the tasks to ensure they could complete the project efficiently and on time.__team__

m) You should check the **layout** of the final draft before submitting, for example, size of margins, font and line spacing.__format__

Task 4: Collocations #1

The following are the collocations:

ethical dilemma, significant portion, gain insight, maximum duration, mutual trust, preliminary findings, qualitative data, domestic sphere, cultural norm, military action

The following is the collocations as per the exercise in the book:

ethical	portion
significant	findings
gain	dilemma
maximum	insight
mutual	data
preliminary	action
qualitative	duration
domestic	norm
cultural	trust
military	sphere

Task 5: Collocations #2

Words which collocate	Additional word from Ex 4	AWL Sublist 9 word
social--	*cultural--*	*norm*
-- force, -- power, -- service	-- action	military
private-- , public--	domestic--	sphere
-- analysis, -- approach, -- method, -- research, -- study	-- data	qualitative
-- recognition, -- support, -- understanding	-- trust	mutual
-- consideration, -- issue, -- principle, -- problem, -- question	-- dilemma	ethical
give -- (into), offer -- (into), provide -- (into)	gain -- (into)	insight
-- data, -- result	-- findings	preliminary
long --, short --	maximum --	duration
large --, small --	significant --	portion

Task 6: Word form #1

a) The student **accommodation** (accommodate) has recently been renovated and is now much more comfortable.

b) The wing of a bat is **analogous** (analogy) to the wing of an insect, although their evolutionary origins are very different.

c) The recent flooding was an **unanticipated** (anticipate) event. It was not expected to happen, and they were not prepared for it.

d) The equipment was very **bulky** (bulk) and difficult to move.

e) The two research groups were working on the same project at the same time, which looked like more than just a **coincidence** (coincide).

f) Those who knew him praised his **devotion** (devote) to the civil rights movement.

g) Climate change is leading to increased levels of coastal **erosion** (erode), which in turn is leading to loss of homes.

h) The **mediation** (mediate) between the two sides led to an acceptable agreement.

i) Despite having great freedom of choice, there is much **passivity** (passive) in how consumers choose new products.

j) The **relaxation/relaxing** (relax) of the regulations did not lead to the expected increase in crime.

k) Although parents may sometimes want to hit their child, they should exercise **restraint** (restrain), since such punishment is harmful.

l) The wall of the apparatus used several layers of hardened plastic to increase **rigidity** (rigid).

m) In addition to his main income, he also derived a **supplementary** (supplement) income from interest on savings.

n) The **unification** (unify) of East and West Germany is one of the defining moments of the late twentieth century.

Task 7: Word form #2

These are the opposites:

unattainable	cease**less**	**in**coherent	**in**compatible
unconfined	**un**controversial	**in**definite*	**un**diminished
unethical	**in**finite	**un**founded	**im**mature
~~**in**visible~~*			

These are the opposites on the prefix/suffix mind map.

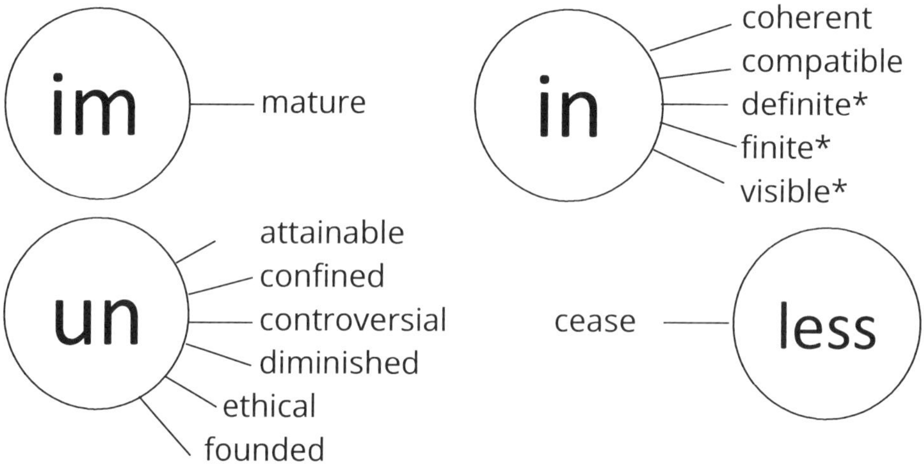

a) His goal was unattainable. He could never hope to reach it.
b) The research experiment was considered to be unethical since it subjected animals to undue cruelty.
c) For some time after suffering a stroke his speech was incoherent. No one could understand him.
d) His views were very uncontroversial and raised no objections.
e) The number of possible sentences in any language is infinite, since words can be put together in endless combinations.
f) The controversial decision led to ceaseless debate at the meeting. It seemed that it would never end.
g) His suspicions were unfounded. There was no evidence whatsoever.
h) The immature young of most mammal species need to be looked after until they are old enough to fend for themselves.
i) His love of research was undiminished despite his age and he still continued to conduct experiments regularly.
j) A(n) indefinite number of people signed up for the study. The experimenters did not have a clear idea of how many there were.
k) Their joy at being awarded the research grant was unconfined.
l) The two parts of the apparatus were incompatible and would not fit together.

Sublist 10

Task 1: Focus on Meaning #1

Stressors, the stimuli that initiate the stress process, can be placed into one of two broad categories: chronic and acute. Chronic stressors include events that **persist** over an extended period of time, such as caring for a parent with dementia, long-term unemployment, or imprisonment. Acute stressors involve brief focal events that sometimes continue to be experienced as overwhelming well after the event has ended, such as falling on an icy sidewalk and breaking your leg (Cohen, Janicki-Deverts, & Miller, 2007). Potential stressors include major traumatic events, significant life changes, daily hassles, as well as other situations in which a person is regularly exposed to threat, challenge, or danger.

Some stressors involve traumatic events or situations in which a person is exposed to actual or threatened death or serious injury. Stressors in this category include exposure to **military** combat, threatened or actual physical assaults (e.g., physical attacks, sexual assault, robbery, childhood abuse), terrorist attacks, natural disasters (e.g., earthquakes, floods, hurricanes), **undergoing** major surgery, and automobile accidents.

Most stressors that we **encounter** are not nearly as *intense* as the ones described above. Many potential stressors we face involve events or situations that require us to make changes in our **ongoing** lives and require time as we adjust to those changes. Examples include death of a close family member, marriage, divorce, moving, and starting a new job. This kind of stress can be both positive and negative. However, most of the available evidence suggests that, at least as far as mental health is concerned, undesirable or negative events are more strongly associated with poor outcomes (such as **depression**) than are desirable, positive events (Hatch & Dohrenwend, 2007).

Potential stressors do not always involve major life events. Daily hassles—the minor irritations and annoyances that are part of our everyday lives (e.g., rush hour traffic, lost keys, unfriendly **colleagues**, inclement weather, arguments with friends or family)—can build on one another and leave us just as stressed as life change events (Kanner, Coyne, Schaefer, & Lazarus, 1981).

Stressors can include situations in which one is frequently exposed to challenging and unpleasant events, such as difficult, demanding, or unsafe working conditions. Although most jobs and occupations can at times be demanding, some are clearly more stressful than others. For example, most people would likely agree that a firefighter's work is **inherently** more stressful than that of a florist. **Likewise**, most would agree that jobs containing various unpleasant elements, such as those requiring exposure to loud noise (heavy equipment operator), those which **pose** a danger to health (healthcare worker during a contagious pandemic), those involving constant harassment and threats of physical violence (prison guard) or perpetual frustration (bus driver in a major city), or those mandating that an employee work alternating day and night shifts (hotel desk clerk), are much more demanding—and thus, more stressful—than those that do not contain such elements.

Task 2: Focus on Meaning #2

a) Productivity in the country has increased steadily over the past three decades, **in spite of** the current global recession.__notwithstanding__
b) Local governments can **impose** their own taxes on local businesses and individuals.__levy__
c) Many **supposed** charities are in fact nothing of the kind, and are making considerable profits for their board members.__so-called__
d) The government has brought in legislation **so that** revenue from ecotourism can be used directly to preserve the environment visited by tourists__whereby__
e) There has been considerable increase economic growth over the past three years, **although** at a slower rate than experts predicted.__albeit__
f) In social science experiments it is sometimes necessary to mislead participants in order to maintain the **soundness** of the experiment.__integrity__
g) In economics, fiat money has no **basic** value, but is declared by a government to be the legal tender of a country.__intrinsic__
h) The somatosensory cortex of the brain is organized topographically, meaning, for example, that part of the cortex that processes information from the hand is **next** to the part that processes information from the wrist.__adjacent__
i) The **soon-to-be published** article on the results of the Covid-19 vaccine is eagerly awaited by government health officials.__forthcoming__
j) The judge chose to **use** the law protecting refugees from being exported back to their own country.__invoke__
k) Although the drug led to a reduction of symptoms in a majority of patients, it was a failure **anyway**, since it had too many side effects.__nonetheless__
l) Due to his expertise in the field, the professor was invited to be part of a **committee** of climate change experts presenting information to businesses.__panel__
m) Although many people hold beliefs that can be considered **strange**, this is different from a delusion, which is a belief that is clearly absurd.__odd__
n) There were many reasons for the **fall** of communist governments at the end of the Cold War.__collapse__

Task 3: Collocations

The following shows the collocations as per the exercise in the book.

encounter	debate/process
enormous	straightforward
fairly/relatively	a challenge/a problem/a question/a threat to
ongoing	difficulties/problems
pose	amount of/impact

a) The rise of armed conflict in the region will **pose a threat** to travellers, who should only go there if absolutely essential.

b) Learning to ride a bicycle is a **fairly/relatively straightforward** task. [*Note: both collocations are fine here.*]

c) His research had a(n) **enormous impact** on future researchers in the field.

d) Many beginning academic writers **encounter difficulties/problems** with collocation use. [*Note: both collocations are fine here.*]

e) There is a(n) **ongoing debate** about whether soft drugs such as marijuana should be legalised.

Task 4: Word Form

a) After the precautions they took to ensure accurate measurements, a large margin of error was **inconceivable** (conceive).

b) The respondents had an **inclination** (incline) to agree with each other when questioned in pairs.

c) Although the report claimed to present new information, it was in fact a **compilation** (compile) of previous, much older research data.

d) They waited for the **assembly** (assemble) of all the participants before they began the meeting.

e) His arguments were **unconvincing** (convince), which meant that nobody believed his theory to be correct.

f) He was **reluctant** (reluctance) to release the results until the trial was complete.

g) One of the effects of prolonged stress is **depression** (depress).

h) Some students give up too easily, and teachers should communicate to them the importance of **persistence** (persist) in learning.

i) He **underwent** (undergo) brain surgery last week in an effort to remove the tumour, though it is unclear if the operation was successful.

k) The did not fully understand the **enormity** (enormous) of the task until they had started, when they realized just how difficult it would be.

Index of words

The following are all the words in sublists 7-10 of the AWL, with page numbers.

Academic Word List: Sublist 7 7
adapt 8
adult 8
advocate 9
aid 9
channel 10
chemical 11
classic 11
comprehensive 12
comprise 12
confirm 13
contrary 13
convert 14
couple 15
decade 15
definite 16
deny 16
differentiate 17
dispose 17
dynamic 18
eliminate 18
empirical 19
equip 19
extract 20
file 21
finite 21
foundation 22
globe 22
grade 23
guarantee 24
hierarchy 25
identical 25
ideology 26
infer 26
innovate 27
insert 27
intervene 28
isolate 28

media 29
mode 29
paradigm 30
phenomenon 30
priority 31
prohibit 31
publication 32
quote 32
release 33
reverse 34
simulate 35
sole 35
somewhat 36
submit 36
successor 37
survive 37
thesis 38
topic 38
transmit 39
ultimate 39
unique 40
visible 41
voluntary 41
Academic Word List: Sublist 8 49
abandon 50
accompany 50
accumulate 51
ambiguous 51
append 52
appreciate 52
arbitrary 53
automate 53
bias 54
chart 54
clarify 55
commodity 55
complement 56
conform 56
contemporary 57
contradict 57
crucial 58
currency 58

denote 59
detect 59
deviate 60
displace 60
drama 61
eventual 61
exhibit 62
exploit 62
fluctuate 63
guideline 63
highlight 64
implicit 64
induce 65
inevitable 65
infrastructure 66
inspect 66
intense 67
manipulate 67
minimise 68
nuclear 68
offset 69
paragraph 69
plus 70
practitioner 70
predominant 71
prospect 71
radical 72
random 73
reinforce 73
restore 74
revise 74
schedule 75
tense 75
terminate 76
theme 76
thereby 77
uniform 77
vehicle 78
via 78
virtual 78
visual 79
widespread 79

Academic Word List: Sublist 9 87
accommodate 88
analogy 88
anticipate 89
assure 89
attain 90
behalf 90
bulk 91
cease 91
coherent 92
coincide 92
commence 93
compatible 93
concurrent 94
confine 94
controversy 95
converse 95
device 96
devote 96
diminish 97
distort 97
duration 98
erode 98
ethic 99
format 99
found 100
inherent 100
insight 101
integral 101
intermediate 102
manual 102
mature 103
mediate 103
medium 104
military 104
minimal 105
mutual 105
norm 106
overlap 106
passive 107
portion 107
preliminary 108

protocol 108
qualitative 109
refine 109
relax 110
restrain 110
revolution 111
rigid 111
route 112
scenario 112
sphere 113
subordinate 113
supplement 114
suspend 114
team 115
temporary 115
trigger 116
unify 116
violate 117
vision 117
Academic Word List: Sublist 10 127
adjacent 128
albeit 128
assemble 129
collapse 129
colleague 130
compile 130
conceive 131
convince 131
depress 132
encounter 132
enormous 133
forthcoming 133
incline 134
integrity 134
intrinsic 135
invoke 135
levy 136
likewise 136
nonetheless 137
notwithstanding 137
odd 138
ongoing 138

panel.....139
persist.....139
pose.....140
reluctance.....140
so-called.....141
straightforward.....141
undergo.....142
whereby.....142

About the author

Sheldon Smith has been teaching English for Academic Purposes (EAP) since 2002, working in the UK, Indonesia and China. Since 2005 he has been working on pathway programmes which prepare EFL students for university study at Western universities, chiefly in the USA, UK and Australia. In addition to text books for academic English, he is the author of several novels and text books for Chinese language learning. He is the founder and chief developer of the EAPFoundation.com website. He currently resides in Guangzhou, Guangdong province, China.

About Evident Press

Evident Press is an independent publisher specialising in academic texts. It currently publishes two series of books for academic English: the *EAP Foundation series*, in conjunction with the acclaimed academic English website EAPFoundation.com; and the *Unlock the Academic Word List* series. It also publishes the *Chinese Characters for HSK* series for learning Chinese.

Accessing Online Resources

All books published by Evident Press include additional online resources. These resources are available free of charge. All you need is an access code (see below).

Follow these steps to access the resources.

1) Go to https://www.evidentpress.com/resources/.
2) To access the resources, you will first need to register. If you have already done this, skip to step 3). If not, click on **Register** and follow the onscreen instructions, which will require you to enter a username, your first name, last name, email address and password.
3) Use your login details to login to the site. This will take you to your **Resources** page. This screen will tell you which books you already have access to, if any.
4) Click on the button **Add Resources**. Enter the access code to gain access to the resources. The code for *EAP Foundation: Academic Presentations* is shown below.

ACCESS CODE: **9hjTt2d**

You will only need to enter this code once. In future when you log in, the resources for this book will automatically show up.

If you follow the above steps, you should be able to access all the resources for the book. If you have any difficulty entering the code, registering or logging in, please contact Evident Press by using the form on the Evident Press contact page, or directly at contact@evidentpress.com.

Printed in Great Britain
by Amazon

57701974R00099